W9-BKL-183

GETTING FIRED
FOR THE GLORY OF GOD

COLLECTED WORDS OF
MIKE YACONELLI
FOR YOUTH WORKERS

ZONDERVAN®

ZONDERVAN.com/
AUTHORTRACKER
follow your favorite authors

youth
specialties

youth specialties

Getting Fired for the Glory of God
Copyright 2008 by Karla Yaconelli

Youth Specialties resources, 300 S. Pierce St., El Cajon, CA 92020 are published by Zondervan, 5300 Patterson Ave. SE, Grand Rapids, MI 49530.

ISBN 978-0-310-28358-4

Cover design by SharpSeven Design
Interior design by David Conn

Printed in the United States of America

08 09 10 11 12 • 18 17 16 15 14 13 12 11 10 9 8 7 6 5 4 3 2 1

CONTENTS

985

119739

INTRODUCTION:
THE ELDER WITH THE
ADOLESCENT HEART

Four years after our dad, Mike Yaconelli, passed away, I stood preparing to deliver a morning talk at a Christian arts festival in England. Gathered around the makeshift stage was a crowd of three to four thousand people. I'd never given a talk in England, and I knew that the people wedged together in the grandstands and grass patches bordering the Cheltenham Racecourse had gathered not because of me, but because of their love for my dad.

Ten minutes into my talk, I noticed three women lying on the grass a few yards away from the stage, their eyes shut. After I finished my talk, a line of people formed to greet me. For almost two hours I stood and listened to people tell stories about my dad and the impact his words and presence had on their lives. Toward the end of this reception line were the women I'd noticed during my talk. They introduced themselves as London youth workers, paused awkwardly, and then confessed what I knew was on everyone's minds that morning.

"We miss your dad terribly. Your voice sounds so much like your father's. After you started speaking, we closed our eyes and listened to your voice. And for a few moments, it was like we were listening to him." Their eyes welled up with tears, they hugged me, and they walked away.

My siblings and I compiled this book for the many youth ministers who continue to seek encouragement, truth-telling, and guidance within Dad's words. The field of youth ministry is populated with educational specialists, developmental theorists, sociologists, and church-growth experts. These people know how to design and organize successful youth ministries. Among these people, Dad is an anomaly.

Although considered a founder and expert on youth ministry, Dad was often the last person to whom you'd want to turn for advice on organizing and establishing a youth ministry program.

Dad was the guy you wanted to go to when you needed kindness, when you needed the truth, when you felt lost and hurt by the church. Dad was the guy to whom youth workers turned when they'd forgotten who they were, when they'd lost track of Jesus, or when they felt plain lonely in their ministries.

Dad was a seeker, a visionary, and an intuitive who could sense the Spirit of God within youth ministry and give words to what he felt. Dad wore his personal and professional frustrations on his sleeve. He was a truth-teller, unafraid of exploring the shadow side of ministry, church life, marriage, childrearing, and Christian living. Dad often claimed that part of his spiritual gift was a built-in "crap detector" that allowed him to notice and expose the lies, the pretending, the feigned humility, and the greed that infects the Christian church. He had a prophetic anger; an impatience with churches, pastors, youth pastors, and Christian celebrities who promoted a kind of perfectionism that left all of us feeling ashamed and discouraged.

Sometimes people found Dad too negative and critical; yet he believed another aspect of his spiritual gift was being a cynic. As he told one youth working audience, "Someone has to balance out all those positive, optimistic Christians."

Dad was almost compulsively creative, looking for original words and unexpected interactions. He wanted to uncover and create a sense of surprise and wonder whenever he was among people. Sometimes this caused him to overstate things (see "The Failure of Youth Ministry," p. 107) or purposely stir things up (see "Youth Ministry Rant," p. 79).

"Be anything but lukewarm," Jesus says to us in Revelation 3:15-16. Dad took these words to heart. He'd rather have a crowd get riled up, yell obscenities, or walk out than just sit and nod their heads in polite agreement. (In this he was successful—and as a result, he received a constant stream of angry and critical letters throughout his life.) He wanted to catch people's attention, shake things up, and force them to think and question. He saw the Christian life as a risky adventure, and nothing upset him more than a Christianity that didn't keep people on the edges of their seats.

Most of the writings here were first published in a column titled "Dangerous Wonder" that Dad wrote for *Youthworker Journal* from 1999 until his death in October 2003. (The July 2001 column—an excerpt from his book *Messy Spirituality*—was omitted.) As you'll see, these columns were soulful, edgy, funny, and often got him into trouble (see "An Apology," p. 111). We've also included "Caring for Your Own Soul While Ministering to Others," an article Dad wrote in 2002 for an in-house publication with Zondervan. In addition to these writings, there are four audio and two video recordings of talks Dad gave to youth working audiences.

Selecting recordings for this book was difficult. First of all, we had to track them down. Dad had no interest in archiving his own life. And although most of his talks over his 40-plus years in ministry were recorded, Dad rarely saved any of these recordings (nor did he keep copies of published articles). He was more interested in what was coming next than in what had already been done. And yet after scavenging Dad's office, garage, glove compartments, and closets, we were able to come up with almost 50 hours of recorded youth ministry talks. Unfortunately, we could track down only one recording from before 1995—a talk given in San Francisco at the closing general session of the 1986 Youth Specialties National Youth Workers Convention—which we've included here. (The sound quality on this cassette isn't perfect, but it was a rare discovery for us.)

As a young man, Dad won the Toastmasters International "World Champion of Public Speaking" award in 1966. He knew how to speak in a way that was both compelling and entertaining. However, as my brother and sisters and I listened to the various seminars and keynotes, we found ourselves drawn to the talks that were less polished, more freewheeling—talks in which Dad was raw and transparent, talks in which you can hear his relationship with the audience. Ultimately, we tried to choose recordings in which Dad's presence, his passion, his quick wit, and his love for youth workers was most accessible. You'll find our own notes and impressions for each of these talks included in the back of the book.

Before you engage in any of this material, however, the first thing you should keep in mind is that Dad loved Jesus. I know all of us within the Christian faith are supposed to love Jesus. Many of us who work in the church try to love Jesus and help others love Jesus. But often a more accurate statement is that we *believe* in Jesus, we have *faith* in Jesus, we struggle to *follow* Jesus. Sometime after Dad turned 50, a transformation took place in his life. He went from believing in, admiring, and following Jesus to just plain loving Jesus.

For his family, those of us most intimate with him, Dad's love for Jesus was often disarming. You might be standing in his kitchen drinking coffee (with potatoes and peppers cooking on the stove), and Dad would start talking about a project he was working on or an insight for a sermon he was preparing. The tone would be light and informal; then all of a sudden, he'd mention the name of Jesus, and his voice would catch. At first you'd stop to see if he was okay, or if he needed something. Then you'd notice his eyes were wet, and he'd look at you kind of helplessly and shake his head for a moment as he tried to hold back the tears. It was then that you remembered: *He really loves Jesus.*

The truth is that Dad's love for Jesus can be easily over-looked—particularly for those of us "professional Christians" who've been trained to treat Jesus as an object lesson, a belief statement, a platitude, or a role model. Dad knew this. He knew how the work of ministry, the bureaucracy of church life, and the flashing lights of culture could obscure the vulnerable love of Jesus. And so through humor and story, rants and raw confessions, he tried to bring youth workers back to their first love—back to the center of the Christian faith—to what he called "the compelling, attractive, demanding, frightening Jesus."

The second thing you should know is that Dad loved youth workers. Speaking to a group of youth ministry volunteers in Canada, he choked up as he tried to help the group feel the unique gift that youth ministers offer the church: "How many adults wake up in the morning and say to themselves, *I wonder if I can find some adolescents to hang out with today?* You do. You're the ones. That's what makes you...weird. And that's what makes you gifted...I hope you realize that whatever you do makes a difference."

Dad appreciated the fact that most youth workers take great risks—often sacrificing financial security, professional status, time with family, self-esteem, and even spiritual well-being. From experience Dad knew there were few rewards in youth ministry, few signs of success. He knew youth ministers often felt beaten down, confused, helpless, underappreciated, patronized, and criticized by parents, church members, pastors, and even teenagers. Dad loved youth workers for their willingness to offer their gifts to God despite a lack of results, demanding parents, dismissive pastors, and angry custodians.

Ultimately, Dad loved youth workers because he encountered Jesus in youth workers—in their passion for God and in their creative abilities to find new ways of bringing the gospel to life for another generation.

If Dad continues to be valued by youth workers, then I believe it's because he carried the spirit of adolescence that's at the heart of youth ministry. In listening to Dad, you'll find the idealism, romanticism, spontaneity, irreverence, and passion that mirror the teenagers we serve, as well as the teenager in all of us. If you listen closely you can hear the yearnings of teenagers within his words and writings: *Where's the passion? Where's the creativity? Where's the dreaming?*

Dad recognized the fact that the church is an "adult" institution, often insensitive to the spirit and gifts of adolescents. Dad also knew that the church, like adulthood, is constantly susceptible to routine, stagnation, self-protection, and security. He knew that in the pursuit of "success" the church was becoming increasingly hesitant to take chances with Jesus— and more likely to stand with the Pharisees in contempt for and in suspicion of the screwed-up, the losers, the messy, and the failed human beings (in other words, all of us) who long for some kind of transforming grace.

And yet Dad's words are valuable not only because they reflect the passion and frustrated yearnings of teenagers, but also because his words ring with an undeniable compassion and concern for others. The great psychoanalyst and developmental theorist Erik Erikson once claimed that there's a deep connection between the adolescent and the elder. More than any other age groups, the young and the old spend significant amounts of time reflecting on death, the meaning of life, the reality of suffering, and the miracle of love.

I believe Dad's impact on the field of youth ministry came not only from the spirit of the teenager within him, but also from the spirit of the elder within him. In Dad's words there is wisdom, experience, and genuine concern for others. Within his spontaneity, creativity, and impatience is a deep and lasting trust in the church, the Bible, and the committed volunteer. This is what gives his humor and criticism depth and relevance. It's the sense that even his most razor-sharp critiques are grounded in a deep love for the church and Jesus' mission of love.

The hope that my brother and sisters and I share in offering this book is that you may find encouragement for your own life and ministry. Our hope is that in reading (or rereading) Dad's words and listening to his voice, you may find a companion who'll help you name the principalities and powers that bind so many of us who work and live within the church. Our hope is that you may find within Dad's writing and speaking a reminder of your own calling to love Jesus and love kids, as well as the courage to follow that calling—even if it means losing your job.

And so our prayer is that as you read and hear these words, you may find yourself led to step outside, lie down in the grass, close your eyes, and draw closer...not to Mike Yaconelli, but to the One who animated Mike Yaconelli's life, the One who gave him meaning and purpose, the One he loved, the One he called Savior, the One who calls to you even now saying, "Come to me, all you who are weary and burdened, and I will give you rest" (Matthew 11:28).

—Mark Yaconelli, along with Trent, Lisa, Jill, and Jessica (Mike's kids)

One last note: Toward the end of Dad's life, he became increasingly concerned about the suffering of children and young people in Africa. In the year before he died, he began giving money and support to various programs in Africa that worked with the many young people who've been orphaned because of AIDS. After Dad's death, our family worked with World Vision to establish a school in Dad's name for children in Zimbabwe. Half of all the royalties from this book will be sent to this school to provide clean water, school supplies, mosquito netting, and other basic necessities. Thanks to you, the ministry continues...

SOULS IN DANGER
(JULY 1999)

In his book *In the Name of Jesus*, Henri Nouwen writes that after 25 years in ministry, "I found myself praying poorly, living somewhat isolated from other people, and very much preoccupied with burning issues...something inside was telling me that my success was *putting my own soul in danger*."

I'm very concerned about the souls of America's youth workers. Youth ministry here is precariously close to collapsing under the weight of its own success. We seem to be caught in the spell of a media-driven, techno-event culture that's dazzling the life out of us. We have a spectacular array of seminars, products, conventions, rallies, crusades, and programs that draw large crowds and make lots of noise—and we wait expectantly for the next spectacular array of events. Sadly, an increasing number of youth workers have opted for *more* instead of *deep*. All over the country, one youth ministry after another is becoming a monument to our charisma, a tribute to our technology, a testimony to our management skills...and one more nail in the body of Jesus.

Our ministry staff meetings are more like management meetings than prayer meetings. We spend our time talking about how to relate to our new computer systems instead of talking about our relationships with Jesus. The modern senior pastor operates like a CEO instead of a spiritual director, mentor, or fellow struggler. Numbers, activities, and programs dominate our agendas, and we soon discover that in today's institutional church, mission statements, strategies, and results matter most. Efficiency and control rule. The *bottom line* is tangible growth. The youth minister's soul is irrelevant. Then we wake up one day with very successful youth programs, only to discover our success has cost us our souls.

A high-profile, parachurch youth ministry approached a veteran youth worker friend of mine and tossed her name in the hat for one of its executive openings. She was excited to be considered for the job and saw the position as a great place to launch a care program for the staff members' souls. In her interview, one executive told her, "I know you're passionate about our staff members and their relationships with God, but frankly, your job will cover a lot of responsibilities. I'm at the same level you'll be. In terms of my job description, *helping staffers with their relationships with God is 27th on my list.*"

No youth ministry, church, or parachurch should survive if the condition of its youth minister's soul is 27th on the list.

Today's youth ministry culture is consumed with *doing* rather than *being*. So many of us know what it means to believe in Jesus—but we don't know what it means to *be* with Jesus. We know how to talk about Jesus—but we don't know how to listen to Jesus talk to *us*. We're experts at doing youth work—but we don't know how to let God work in our hearts. We know much about saving souls—but we have no clue about soul making. We're comfortable with God's people—but uncomfortable when we're alone with God.

We've forgotten the *real* bottom line: Our souls. Let's reclaim them. Let's start with our relationships with Jesus. Let's start the new millennium by reaching inside our souls before we try to reach the world. Let's start at the feet of Jesus and go from there.

1. STAFF MEETINGS. Let's begin our pilgrimage with Jesus by changing the way we do business. Let's make intimacy with Jesus our business. Let's suggest to our church staffs that we spend the majority of our meeting times talking about our relationships with God. Let's spend that time praying and paying attention to what God is doing.

2. YOUTH STAFF. Instead of starting with what we're *doing* with the kids, let's spend our meetings talking about *who we are* to the kids. Maybe we can cut back on activities and spend more time together in silence and solitude so our young people can sense the presence of Christ in our staffs.

3. IRRELEVANCE. Think of all the hours you and your staffs spend programming. What if that time were spent being "irrelevant" by seeking God's presence, listening to God's voice, looking at God's beauty, tasting God's Word, and resting in him? Maybe in the frenzy of modern culture, the most relevant thing youth workers can do is cling to Jesus— so those who're scurrying from one cultural icon to another will trip over him on their way toward relevance.

It isn't easy to stay with Jesus in ministry...but we must. Deep in our souls, he's whispering how much he loves us. If we'd just take the time to listen to those words and believe them, then our ministries would be gloriously ruined by Jesus—and our souls would no longer be in danger.

A FREEDOM STORY
(SEPTEMBER 1999)

In his book *The Easy Yoke*, Doug Webster retells a great Will Willimon story about a young, idealistic college student who ended up in one of the worst-looking housing projects in Philadelphia.

A brand-new Christian, this wide-eyed urban missionary didn't have a clue how to evangelize in the middle of the city. Frightened and anxious to share his new faith, the young man approached a very large, intimidating tenement house. Cautiously making his way through the dark, cluttered hallways, he walked up a flight of stairs and heard a baby crying. The baby was inside one of the apartments. He knocked on the door and was met by a woman holding a naked baby. She was smoking, and she wasn't in the mood to hear about Jesus. She cursed at the boy and slammed the door. The young man was devastated. He walked outside, slumped down on the street curb, and cried. *Look at me,* he said to himself. *How in the world could someone like me think I could tell anyone about Jesus?*

Then the young man looked up and saw a dilapidated old store on the corner. It was open, and he went inside and walked around. It was then that he remembered the baby in the tenement was naked and that the woman was smoking. So he bought some diapers and a pack of cigarettes and headed back to the woman's apartment. He knocked on the door, and before the woman could start cursing him, he slid the cigarettes and diapers inside the open door.

The woman invited him in.

The student played with the baby. He put a diaper on the baby—even though he'd never put a diaper on a baby before. And when the woman asked him to smoke, he smoked—even though he'd never smoked before. He spent the whole day playing with the baby, changing diapers, and smoking.

Late in the afternoon the woman asked him, "What's a nice college boy like you doing in a place like this?" He told her all he knew about Jesus. Took him about five minutes. When he stopped talking, the woman looked at him and said, "Pray for me and my baby that we make it out of here alive." He prayed.

This young man's story is a freedom story. Because of his freedom in Christ, he was led by the Holy Spirit to change diapers and, well...smoke. If this young man were in your youth group and gave this testimony, I have a strong feeling many Christians wouldn't be celebrating his freedom in Christ—they'd be asking you what was going to be done about his "indiscretion."

Trouble is, what he did was a Spirit-led indiscretion. Paul said it best: "Where the Spirit of the Lord is, there is freedom" (2 Corinthians 3:17). And in this situation, he was free to smoke.

Uh oh. When Jesus says the truth sets us free, he isn't kidding.

The trouble with modern Christianity is that we've tried to de-fang the truth. Freedom in Christ does have fangs. Sharp ones. That's why when Christ was around, people weren't afraid to tear roofs apart and let little children run out of control. The freedom that Jesus proclaims isn't a nice, religious concept or a cute idea—it's a wild, dangerous, shocking, upsetting, uncomfortable, daring, threatening truth. Freedom in Christ means we are free to fail and free not to fail; we are free to follow Christ and free to run from him; we are free to obey and free not to obey; we are free to sin and free not to sin.

Freedom in Christ makes us all extremely nervous. It should! Because freedom in Christ isn't a youth ministry issue, it's a *soul* issue. Although the Spirit of God calls us to freedom, many of us have allowed our bosses, our churches, and our parents to quench the Spirit and kill the life within us. Then, instead of following Christ, we start following policy, parental expectations, and staff directives. And suddenly we find ourselves exhausted, burned out—our souls lifeless and dead.

Freedom in Christ is very hazardous to our jobs, too. It means we're more afraid of disappointing Jesus than we are of being fired. Freedom in Christ means we have the courage to ask why our staff meetings are about church business instead of about Jesus.

Freedom is a wonderfully risky consequence of listening to the wild whispers of Christ's Holy Spirit and sharing those whispers with our students.

"Are you tired?" Jesus asks. "Worn out? Burned out on religion? Come to me. Get away with me and you'll recover your life. I'll show you how to take a real rest. Walk with me and work with me—watch how I do it. Learn the unforced rhythms of grace. I won't lay anything heavy or ill-fitting on you. Keep company with me and *you'll learn to live freely and lightly*" (Matthew 11:28-30, *The Message*, emphasis added).

What is Jesus whispering to you? Are you too busy? Then slow down. Quit programming so much. Quit trying to fix everybody. Take time to savor Jesus' love for you—and let him run freely in your youth group and in your soul.

THE SINS OF YOUTH MINISTRY
(NOVEMBER 1999)

Sinning is part of adolescence. Sinning is the natural consequence of young people rebelling and finding their way.
That's why youth workers talk a lot about sin. We're good
at warning young people about the dangers of sin. We talk
a lot about abortion, alcohol, drugs, sex, pornography—and
we should. And even more than warning kids away from sin,
Jesus' admonition to his disciples makes it clear that we're
not to cause any of them to sin.

What if our *ministries* cause little ones to sin? What if our
programs cause little ones to sin?

Think that's ridiculous? I wonder.

See if the following tendencies feel familiar...

OVERSIMPLIFICATION

When we tell young people that Jesus is the answer to all our problems, when we paint the world as black-and-white, when we make following Jesus an either-or proposition, when we suggest that young people "just pray, then everything will be all right," when we promise that Jesus always makes us happy and always gives us what we want, we cause little ones to sin.

We know life is much more complicated than "take two Jesus pills and call me in the morning." If we're honest, we'll admit that not everyone who follows Jesus is happy, fulfilled, or has it all together. Surely we understand that prayer is much more complex than simply requesting and receiving. Even asking "What would Jesus do?" isn't all that simple—because often we don't *know* what Jesus would do!

When we promise that life with Jesus is simple, we set up our students for failure. When we adults run off and have affairs, what do our students do then? When their senior pastor is caught abusing little children, what are our students supposed to think then? How do we communicate the harsh, complicated, difficult, wonderful reality that Jesus really is worth following—even when life is blurry, confusing, and difficult?

MANIPULATION

If I witness one more Jesus cheer, if I hear one more "let's have a hand/round of applause/praise offering for Jesus," if I have to endure one more pep rally for Jesus, I'm returning my youth ministry ID card. Because as much as we criticize and complain about our media-ravaged society, as much as we rant about the evils of MTV and pop culture, we've imitated them by rushing to create the world's biggest youth events.

At these events we parade around and glorify all things "beautiful"—the dazzling musicians, the laser shows, the foxes and studs for Jesus. At these events we mesmerize young people with how "cool" Jesus is. These pep rallies give teenagers the illusion that God is cool, that God is winning, that God is the majority—and that their youth ministries and youth leaders are cool, too. But what these events don't dare say is that even cool, dazzling, "beautiful" youth workers are screwed up, broken, and constantly in need of God's grace.

So rather than cheering our young people into the kingdom, maybe we should point them to the broken, inconsistent, *un*cool followers of Jesus in the Bible. Maybe we need to stop pressuring our young people to cheer—just long enough to prepare them for a world in which the real heroes are powerless, tiny, and considered insignificant.

The radical, ugly truth? Jesus was killed by the very people who threw him a pep rally the week before.

SELF-DECEPTION

What characterizes followers of Christ is that we tell the truth. I'm not talking about doctrinal truth—I'm talking *truth*

truth: Where we talk about our strengths and weaknesses; where we talk about our victories and defeats; where we talk about our successes and failures; where we talk about our answers and doubts; where we talk about our joys and depressions; where we talk about our courage and fear.

We talk about *all* of life. We're not afraid that teenagers will see life as a struggle every day—and that it will always be so. Most of all, we point them away from us and toward Jesus. We decrease while Jesus increases.

What's so disturbing about youth ministry today, however, is how little truth-telling there is.

I've been in youth ministry for 40 years, and I wish I could have some of those years to live over again. Oh, God, forgive me for causing your little ones to sin. Oh, God, help me to learn from my mistakes. Oh, God, in spite of me, cause all of your little ones to run into your arms.

Oh, God, help us all.

WHAT WOULD JESUS SAY?
(JANUARY 2000)

Me: "Hey, Jesus!"

Jesus: "Hey."

Me: "I'm a youth worker."

Jesus: "I know. I'm Jesus—remember?"

Me: "Okay. Okay. But...um...why did you make me do youth ministry?"

Jesus: "I didn't 'make' you do youth ministry; I called you."

Me: "Yeah, right. *Called* might as well be the same as *made*. I mean, you made it so I wouldn't be happy doing anything else. You ruined all the other options, Jesus."

Jesus: "You're welcome."

Me: (sigh) "Here's the deal: If you wanted me to do this youth worker thing, then you must believe youth ministry is pretty important."

Jesus: "I do."

Me: "Well, how come the adults in church don't believe it's that important? And have you looked at the pay scale lately? We're always at the bottom of the priority list."

Jesus: "I can relate to that."

Me: "And all they want me to be is a recreation director. You know…plan nice activities and keep their kids from drinking, doing drugs, and getting pregnant."

Jesus: "They believe youth ministry is about making young people nice?"

Me: "Well, yeah. I mean, they believe you're a nice guy and everything—and they want their kids to be like you."

Jesus: "Look, these parents believe I'm a nice *idea*. They believe I care about what *they* care about. They want me to be an enhancement to their lifestyles—and they don't want me making their kids uncomfortable with their lifestyles. Basically, they believe I died on a cross to help their kids get good SAT scores, be captains of football teams and cheerleading squads, and have nice lives. They believe I want to help their children become good Americans. Yuck!"

Me: "I didn't think Jesus would say 'Yuck!'"

Jesus: "It's a Greek word."

Me: "Oh. But aren't Christians supposed to be nice?"

Jesus: "You believe I died on a cross to make people nice? You believe I want to be relegated to the status of *motivational speaker*? Listen, I don't even like football, and I definitely don't like nice people. Look at my disciples! Talk about loud, obnoxious, rude, and flaky—hey, these guys were anything but nice. Remember when 'Mr. Nice Guy' John wanted me to send fire down on a little Samaritan village because they wouldn't let us stay for the night?

"Start telling parents their sons and daughters should take a year after high school and do missions work in South Africa, and see how long you last. Tell them it isn't a good decision to make their kids go to soccer camp instead of church camp, and see how supportive they'll be. Truth is, I came to ruin people's lives—just like I ruined yours. I came to turn people's lives upside down. Remember all that stuff I said about being a sword and turning parents against children? I wasn't kidding."

Me: "But if I let you start ruining kids' lives, we might lose some of them."

Jesus: "Good."

Me: "How can you say 'good'?! Look, I'm beginning to wonder if you're really Jesus."

Jesus: "Why?"

Me: "Why? Because everybody knows youth ministry is about reaching as many students as possible. We've been trying to reach every student for Christ by the year 2000! I mean, this year we're going to have rallies and crusades nationwide with more than 100,000 kids at each of them. We're going to link the entire world by satellite. We're going to have the largest crowds ever!"

Jesus: "I don't like crowds."

Me: "You don't like crowds?!? What are you talking about?!"

Jesus: "I don't like crowds. Go back and read my story. Yes, I had crowds from time to time, but most of the people in them just wanted more wine, food, and power. Then—when I didn't give them what they wanted—they killed me. Nope. I don't like crowds. Besides, my best work was done one-on-one. You know...the woman at the well, the crazy guy, the blind man, the woman caught in adultery. That's when I did my best stuff."

Me: "But...um...that isn't very efficient."

Jesus: "I know. I don't believe in efficiency."

Me: "What?!?"

Jesus: "Let me put it this way: I believe in making disciples one at a time. Very slow stuff."

Me: "But Jesus, I thought you were into 'fast.'"

Jesus: "Nope. I'm about slow. And small."

Me: "Oh, man. If I keep listening to you, I'm going to be fired!"

Jesus: "Good for you."

Me: "Good for me?!? Uh, Jesus, it's not that easy!"

Jesus: "I didn't say it would be easy. I said it would be hard."

Me: "But hard is...well...*hard*."

Jesus: "Tell me about it."

GIRL, INTERRUPTED
(MARCH 2000)

Efrem Smith is a youth worker at Park Avenue Church in Minneapolis, Minnesota. Park Avenue is a legendary urban church that has refused to run to the suburbs; Efrem has refused to run from the dangerous, exhausting demands of youth ministry in the city.

Recently he told me about an experience he had while speaking at a youth conference. He had arrived there tired, weary of speaking. The weeks preceding the conference had been hectic and busy. He was conscious of his dry soul. He felt very distant from God and vulnerable to the common temptations of a youth speaker—arrogance, pride, and total reliance on his gifts.

After the first evening's talk, Efrem—exhausted and looking forward to returning to his room—asked the young people to come forward if they really wanted to be a "revolution-ary for Christ." A number of students responded and were prayed for.

But one girl remained. Her name was Krystal, and she wouldn't leave. She said she had been running from God's call on her life, and she needed more prayer. "The other adult leaders and I kept praying even though it was time to move on to the next event on the schedule," Efrem recalled. "But she kept praying, and we kept praying. Some of the leaders were getting restless. Then, without warning, Krystal stood up and announced, 'I've been running from what I'm supposed to do!' She immediately walked over to a group of young people and began to pray for them. It wasn't just praying, though—it was more like a *prophecy*. She told them how God was going to use them in a powerful way—but her praying was unusual. She prayed about the kids in that group as if she knew them, knew their pasts. It was clear to me that her knowledge came from God. And the more Krystal prayed, the more each student realized something mysterious and holy was going on. One by one, they began to cry. The room was electric with God's presence! People were afraid and awed at the same time. I know I was.

"After praying for everyone in the room, Krystal went out-side and started laying hands on any students she ran into. The longer this went on, the more uncomfortable the adult leaders became. *Why is she doing this? This is weird! When is she going to stop? How am I going to explain this to parents when I get home? She's just doing this to get attention!*

"An hour later I walked into the cafeteria to get some hot chocolate, and there was Krystal, still praying with some of the kids. When she saw me, she came running, laid her hands on me, and began to pray. Now I was uncomfortable. Now I thought she'd gone too far—until I started listening to her prayer: *Oh God, help Efrem to spend more time with his family and with you. Help him to not rely on his gifts alone, but to trust in you. Keep him humble and help him to stand strong against the Devil's attacks.*

"This was no ordinary prayer. Krystal wasn't speaking her words; she was speaking the words of God. She was being *prophetic*. She had no idea how all of us, including me, would respond to her gift. This girl was dangerous!"

Efrem was right. This girl was already dangerous to the status quo, she was already dangerous to the camp schedule, and she'd soon be considered dangerous by the parents of the other kids.

What concerns me about modern youth ministry is the absence of dangerous students like Krystal. We say we believe the gospel is dangerous, but we don't really mean it...do we? We actually mean the gospel is dangerous in a limited context—for non-Christians, school administrators, and liberals. We certainly don't mean that Christianity is dangerous for us, for the church, or for parents.

Think about it. What if we had a room full of Krystals in our youth groups? What if youth group was a place where students diligently sought God's voice in their lives? What if youth group was a sanctuary, not a stage; a worship center, not a program center; a listening place, not a lecturing place?

I know, I know. It's just not practical, not sensible, and not compatible with job security and economic stability. But you and I both know the call of the gospel has never been compatible with economic stability and job security. Then why can't we let Jesus loose on our students?

Here's my answer for *me*: I'm afraid people will think I'm weird, crazy, strange, odd, and fanatical. I can handle almost any reaction from people except the thought that I'm crazy and out of touch with reality. That's my deepest fear.

Yes, I do believe that youth ministry should be the most dangerous place in the church. Yes, I do believe that when Christ runs loose in the youth group, everyone in the church is in danger. I'm convinced that when young people bump into Jesus, they'll leave the comfortable kind of Christianity in which people are normal and predictable—and run after the abnormal and unpredictable Jesus.

I just wish more of us would have the courage to respond to the wild voice of God in our lives—just like that crazy Jesus.

RUN FOR YOUR SOUL!
(MAY 2000)

Recently I was talking to a youth minister about her church, which she described as a constant center of ministry and activity. While in awe of all that church was doing, I wondered what price the staff was paying.

"Oh," she said, "all of us on staff work 70 to 90 hours a week. When we were hired, it was explained to us that the time is short and that those who want to be in God's ministry need to be committed. One of the board members told me, 'We can rest when we get to heaven.'"

I didn't reply. I was stunned.

My silence made the moment noticeably awkward. Finally I said, "Sounds to me like your minister is a workaholic."

"No," she replied defensively, "he just has a real missionary heart."

"No," I said impulsively, "he's definitely a workaholic."

She changed the subject, but I haven't been able to shake our conversation. In this age of the megachurch, our culture worships *doing*. We put busy people on pedestals—especially if the busyness results in *bigger* and *more*.

But when you take the pagan worship of busyness and add to it the biblical mandate to reach the world, you have a lethal combination. The church has baptized busyness and activity and basically formed a pact with the Devil. This pact has succeeded in silencing those who criticize the trend toward hectic, overworked, burned out, spiritually dry ministers who—in the "name of God"—neglect their families, their souls, and their physical well-being.

If I can be so audacious as to "blaspheme" the Gospel of Growth, I respectfully suggest this modern rush to urgency is not only wrong, it's arrogance gone mad.

The moment we believe the kingdom of God is dependent on you or me, we've either experienced a schizophrenic episode, or we've misunderstood our roles as Christians.

Yes, we are to be salt and light. Yes, we are to "go into all the world." Yes, we are to "make disciples." But last time I checked, it took Jesus three years of concentrated effort to make 12 disciples—and it took them the rest of their lives to understand what discipleship means. Last time I checked, Paul suggests we are *in* Christ, not working *for* him.

If you're a youth worker in a church in which the Gospel of Growth rules, RUN! If your senior minister is a winsome, captivating, entrepreneurial workaholic, grab your soul and get out before it's too late.

But when you blow the whistle on the workaholic or rebel against the Gospel of Growth or suggest that God might be calling you to stop adding more activities and people and start growing the ones you have, your very commitment to Christ is questioned. Then you're isolated, criticized, told you're not a "team player"—and finally condemned.

Desperate to find someone who'll tell you you're not crazy, you find no one in the church who will stand with you and refuse to bow to the altar of Growth.

But now you have someone to stand with you.

I'm telling you that you're not crazy. You're not lazy. You're not uncommitted.

And by the way, before the disciples of evangelism start shouting about the need to evangelize now, may I remind you of how many times Jesus said to the people he healed, "Don't tell anyone. Keep your mouth shut" (Matthew 8:4; Mark 7:36, 8:26, 9:9; Luke 5:14, 8:56). Not only did he tell those he healed to keep quiet, but he also told his own disciples on numerous occasions not to tell anyone (Matthew 16:20; Mark 8:30, 9:9; Luke 9:21).

Obviously evangelism is an important goal and calling of the church. But evangelism is not a justification for busyness, exhaustion, burnout, or the destruction of families. Many evangelistic missionary organizations have a reputation for leaders who've burned themselves out on the altar of evangelism. And then—when these charismatic, driven leaders collapse under the weight of their maddening schedules—they're tossed aside for the next leaders who'll also self-destruct.

Youth workers, you haven't been called to crazy, maddening schedules. You haven't been called to reach every student for Christ. You haven't been called to fix all the kids in your youth groups. The weight of your youth groups isn't on your shoulders. Your calling is to be faithful to Christ and to your families—and to reach those you can. Growth is not the gospel. *More* and *bigger* are not fruits of the Spirit.

A few suggestions:

1. Ask that your staff meetings be changed to talk about Jesus and your souls rather than business.

2. As part of your job description, ask for one day a week to spend on your soul—away from the office.

3. Ask for a personal resource budget so you can read books that will help keep your soul intact.

4. As part of your job description, ask for a week every two months to spend alone, in silence, praying and reading and resting.

5. If your senior pastor is a workaholic who can't understand anyone who isn't a workaholic, quit and find a new job.

WHERE'S JESUS?
(JULY 2000)

By the twenty-first chapter of John's Gospel, the risen Jesus has appeared to his disciples on two occasions. But here, seven of his followers are in a quandary. (They *still* don't get it—encouraging, huh?) Frustrated and discouraged, they decide to do the typical "guy thing."

They go fishing.

It's what they know best. It's what's familiar. Better yet—it's seemingly a total waste of time. Just a group of buddies hanging out all night, telling fish stories, reminiscing about when Jesus was around, talking about what they're going to do now. (Luckily there wasn't a church board there to evaluate how they were spending their time.)

But it isn't all goofing around. A couple of the guys on the boat are still good fishermen. They know this lake like the backs of their hands—where the fish are, all the primo spots. So they stay out the entire night, and what do they catch?

Nothing. Absolutely nothing.

What a bunch of losers.

Or were they?

While they're still in the boat, a voice breaks the morning silence: "Hey there! Haven't you any fish?" A man is standing on the shore, directly in front of the sun, his silhouette dark, his features difficult to discern. Not understanding why, the disciples respond in tense unison, "No!"

Without hesitation the man yells back, "Throw your net on the right side of the boat and you will find some!" Within seconds, their net fills with a truckload of fish.

John knows what's going on. The full net of fish has Jesus written all over it. "It is the Lord!" he yells.

Peter, in very Peter-like fashion, jumps in the water and swims for the beach. The rest of the disciples row like crazy to be with Jesus. Why? Because they all realize at that moment that boats don't matter, nets don't matter, and fish don't matter.

You know what *did* matter? Nothing.

That's right. Nothing.

Turns out that catching no fish, getting no results, and wasting hours of time was exactly what the disciples needed to recognize Jesus. They'd been frustrated, confused, angry, exhausted, and unable to get in touch with what they needed. They'd been lonely, afraid, and disillusioned. But this night of "nothing" had prepared the disciples for the "something" (or the Someone) they needed. Now they were ready to receive what Jesus wanted to give them—more time with him.

Jesus didn't care about the big catch of fish—he cared about the guys on the boat. Jesus didn't want to teach his disciples more stuff—he wanted to spend more time with them. He didn't say to his disciples, "Go!"—he said, "Come and have breakfast with me."

Jesus just wanted to have breakfast with his friends, one more time. He just wanted to tell stories together, one more time. Jesus loved his disciples. He loved spending time with them. You see, Jesus understood then—and he understands now—how easy it is to substitute programs, results, and ministry for him.

When our ministries are going well, and when they're going poorly, the question should always be the same: *Where's Jesus?*

I was recently hit with that very question during a meeting with a well-known evangelist. After an hour and a half of his very organized presentation on a new, nationwide program for spreading the gospel, he stopped and asked some of us to respond.

I started to speak, but the words caught in my throat. My tears ambushed me, and I was unable to respond. Taken by surprise, I wondered what my tears were all about. Instantly I saw the following mental picture: A man was leaning against the wall a few feet from us. He seemed lonely and sad, like a wallflower at a dance. One look at his eyes, and I could tell he desperately wanted us to notice him, to pay attention to him, to talk to him—but we just went on with our business and ignored him.

That man was Jesus, of course. There he stood in the midst of our long conversation about strategies, programs, and target markets, and we didn't even notice the very reason why we have these meetings in the first place!

I believe that in much of modern youth ministry, the question "Where's Jesus?" has been replaced with "Who needs Jesus?" I'm really worried that youth ministry itself is drowning out Jesus' constant invitation to us to come have breakfast with him.

I honestly believe that Jesus would love to see *nothing* happening in youth groups across the country. I honestly believe Jesus would love to hear youth workers from all over say to their pastors, parents, and board members, "Oh, sorry! I can't hear about your new program right now—I never miss my breakfast with Jesus."

He's on the shore right now. Just waiting.

TEN EASY STEPS TO GUARANTEE A SUCCESSFUL YOUTH MINISTRY!
(SEPTEMBER 2000)

1. DUMB DOWN THE GOSPEL. Employ attractive phrases such as, "Since I've known Jesus, I'm happier, getting better grades, and captain of the football team!" Even better, reduce the complexity of the gospel into group cheers (e.g., "Give me a J!") or simple worship choruses such as, "God is so good...blah blah blah." (Try singing those words in Ethiopia.) Or even better, try out some hip slang (e.g., God is "phat"; Jesus is a "hottie").

2. COUNT. Constantly make everyone aware of your group's attendance figures and the increases in attendance. Make numbers an issue by setting attendance goals for each activity and reward the group for reaching those goals. Spend lots of time throwing pies at the leaders if goals are reached.

3. PUT YOUR STUDENTS ON DISPLAY. As soon as kids become Christians or rededicate their lives or show real growth, put them in front of the group and have them share their testimonies—*especially if they're physically attractive.* Let young people talk about their faith as much as possible and don't worry about the fact that most young people have no clue how complicated and rough the real world is, with or without Jesus.

4. DON'T ALLOW DOWN TIME. Hey, kids today are MTV kids! They can't sit still for any length of time. Silence, solitude, prayer, meditation, fasting? All *totally* lame in the eyes of this generation! Nope, keep 'em busy, active, noisy, and shuttling from one Christian rock concert to another. Fill every moment of your program with something to do— otherwise you'll lose their attention (which would be disastrous because then they'd have to pay attention to God and their souls).

5. STAY ON THE TECHNOLOGICAL CUTTING EDGE. What would Jesus do? Are you kidding? Jesus would have the best sound system you ever heard, along with a DVD player, the Internet, instant messaging, the coolest Web site, and of course a digital TV. Show your kids that when it comes to the latest technology, Christians are right there! I mean, who needs to read when you can watch?

6. CREATE CELEBRITIES. Make sure your young people get an earful and an eyeful of the latest Christian music stars, video stars, and NFL players who profess their faith in Jesus on national television. Encourage your young people to worship, idolize, and live under the illusion that these people are somehow better, deeper, more Christian, more together, and more dedicated than they are. Let them believe that the marketed images of these celebrities are completely representative of them—even though you know it isn't true.

7. LET YOUTH GROUP TAKE THE PLACE OF CHURCH. Oh sure, encourage your kids to attend the contemporary service—even though you know most of them never will because church is "boring," filled with "dull old people," and the music "sucks." Whatever you do, though, don't suggest that worshiping with people they don't like and connecting with people who are older and wiser just might save them when their adolescent view of the world is shattered. Just keep convincing your students that youth group is a good substitute for church.

8. TOE THE PARENTAL LINE. Whatever you do, don't cause friction with parents by suggesting to their kids that grades, SAT scores, financial security, college degrees, and athletic scholarships really don't matter. Just accept the fact that most parents want their children to attend youth group as long as it doesn't interfere with hockey, football, ice-skating, tennis, ballet, or baseball practice. And don't encourage young people to resist their parents' attempts to smother the call of God on their lives, either. After all, you could get fired!

9. IGNORE THE ARTS. Never encourage painting, dance, sculpture, writing, poetry, ballet, or trips to the museum, symphony, and opera. Stick with activities that rock! The WWF rules!

10. LIVE IN THE NOW. Verify the success of your ministry by visible, measurable, observable results you can access *now*. Don't waste your time worrying about *lasting* results. Who can wait?! Go for the instant return. Hey, once your kids leave youth group, you aren't responsible for what happens to them anyway, right?

11. "US" VERSUS "THEM." (Yeah, yeah, I know I said "Ten Steps"—sue me.) Convince your kids that the only way Christians can make a difference is through public, physical confrontation with the "world." Explain that this "world" is "them" and Christians—the good guys—are "us." And since it's us against them, we have to "stand up for our faith." Encourage them to march in rallies, wear slogan-filled T-shirts, hang banners, and do whatever it takes to get in the world's face. Convince them that the Devil and his demons are running around, wreaking havoc—and the only way to deal with the Devil is to confront and "bind him." Don't let them believe that evil is much more seductive, much more camouflaged and tricky than they could ever imagine. And whatever you do, don't start getting into Jesus' strategy of powerlessness.

Now go get 'em!

"PLEASE SAY GOODBYE TO JESUS FOR ME"
(NOVEMBER 2000)

Every month the youth group at River Road Church visited Holcomb Manor, a local nursing home, to do the church services for the people who stayed there. Daryl Jenkins, a reluctant youth group volunteer and former alcoholic, didn't like nursing homes and had avoided the services. But because of a flu epidemic, Daryl was asked to join a depleted group of sponsors to help with the monthly service. He agreed to go as long as he didn't have to be part of the program.

The day of the service, Daryl felt awkward and out of place. While the service was in progress, Daryl leaned against the back wall, between two residents in wheelchairs. Just as the service finished and Daryl thought about a quick exit, someone grabbed his hand. Startled, Daryl looked down to see a very old man in a wheelchair holding on to his hand tightly. The man was frail and obviously lonely. What could Daryl do but hold his hand back? Oliver Leak was his name, his 91-year-old frame bent and twisted, his face covered with deep wrinkles, and his mouth open most of the time. Oliver's face was expressionless, and Daryl doubted whether the man could hear or see anything.

As everyone began to leave, Daryl realized he didn't want to leave the old man—he'd been left too many times in his long life. Confused by his feelings, Daryl leaned over to Oliver and whispered, "I'm...uh...sorry. I have to leave, *but I'll be back*. I promise." Without any warning, Mr. Leak responded by squeezing Daryl's hand and then let go. Daryl's eyes filled with tears, and he grabbed his stuff and started to leave. Inexplicably, Daryl heard himself say to the old man, "I love you." *(Where did that come from? What's the matter with me?)*

Daryl came back the next month...and the month after that. The routine was the same: Daryl would stand in the back, Mr. Leak would grab his hand, Daryl would say he had to leave, Mr. Leak would squeeze his hand, and Daryl would say softly, "I love you, Mr. Leak." (He had learned his name, of course.) Soon Daryl would find himself looking forward to visiting his old friend.

On Daryl's sixth visit, he could tell something was wrong. Mr. Leak wasn't at the service. Daryl wasn't too concerned at first because it often took the nurses a long time to wheel everyone out. But as the service went on, Daryl became alarmed. He went to the head nurse. "Um, I don't see Mr. Leak here today. Is he okay?" The nurse asked Daryl to follow her, and she led him to Room 27 where Oliver lay in his bed, his eyes closed, his breathing uneven. At 40 years of age, Daryl had never seen someone dying, but he knew Oliver was near death. Slowly Daryl walked to the side of the bed and grabbed Oliver's hand. Oliver was unresponsive, and it didn't take long for the tears to come for Daryl. They had never spoken, and Daryl knew he might never see Oliver alive again. So much he wanted to say, but the words wouldn't come out. They were together about an hour when the youth director gently interrupted Daryl to say they were leaving.

Daryl stood to leave and squeezed Mr. Leak's hand for the last time. "I'm sorry, Oliver, I have to go. I love you." As he unclasped his hand, he felt a squeeze. The tears were unstoppable now. Daryl stumbled toward the door, trying to gain his composure.

A young woman was standing at the door, and Daryl almost bumped into her. "I'm sorry," he said, "I didn't see you."

"It's all right. I've been waiting to see you," she said. "I'm Oliver's granddaughter. He's dying, you know."

"Yes, I know."

"I wanted to meet you," she went on. "When the doctors said he was dying, I came immediately. We were very close. They said he couldn't talk, but he always talked to me. Not much, but I knew what he was saying. Last night he woke up. His eyes were bright and alert. He looked straight into my eyes and said, 'Please say goodbye to Jesus for me,' and he lay back down and closed his eyes. I whispered to him, 'Grandpa, I don't need to say goodbye to Jesus. You're going to be with him soon, and you can tell him hello.' He struggled to open his eyes again, but this time his face lit up with a mischievous smile that he only gave to me, and he said as clearly as I'm talking to you, 'I know, but Jesus comes to see me every month, and he might not know I've gone.' He closed his eyes and hasn't spoken since.

"I told the nurse what he said, and she told me about you coming every month, holding his hand. I wanted to thank you for him, for me, and...well...I never thought of Jesus being as chubby and bald as you, but I imagine Jesus is very glad to have been mistaken for you. I know Oliver is. Thank you." She leaned over and kissed Daryl on the forehead. Oliver Leak died peacefully the next morning.

May God give us more volunteers like Daryl Jenkins.

HURRIED DISCIPLESHIP
(JANUARY 2001)

I don't believe in discipleship.

Got your attention yet?

What I mean is I don't believe in the way discipleship is communicated and practiced with most youth groups today.

I disagree with the popular practice of involving young people in an intense regimen of Bible study, prayer, worship, leadership, evangelism, and accountability where young people are challenged to "take the campus for Christ," "be radical for Jesus," and "give 110 percent."

I know, I know. How could any Bible-believing Christian not believe in a youth ministry that encourages young people to be "on fire for Jesus"?

Well, of course I'm in favor of young people knowing Jesus. What I'm not in favor of is young people *doing* Jesus, because what most youth-oriented discipleship programs are about is *doing*—reading the Bible, praying, worshiping, attending, leading, and evangelizing with no mention of intimacy, waiting, listening, noticing, and paying attention.

Youth-oriented discipleship programs have reduced disciples to cheerleaders and political organizers. Discipleship has been turned into a measurable, external activity instead of an immeasurable, internal lack of activity. Spending time evangelizing has replaced spending time with Jesus, and sharing our faith with others has replaced growing in our faith with Jesus. But there's another, more serious problem.

Young people are...well...young, which means they're immature, confused by their hormones, inexperienced, naive, and idealistic. None of these qualities is "bad"; in fact, they're wonderful gifts of youth that are needed in the church, but they aren't neutral. Simply put, discipleship is a lifelong process, not a youth activity.

Remember when you were a little child, and you dressed up in your parents' clothes? Such antics were cute, but clearly the clothes didn't fit. Young people are being asked to dress up like disciples, but the clothes don't fit.

How could they? The Bible was written by adults—grown-ups who'd lived long lives, who'd suffered greatly for their faith—and the conclusions they reached were squeezed out of pain and heartbreak and failure. Yet we impose our adult views of discipleship on young people who couldn't possibly understand what it all means. They haven't lived long enough.

But in a culture in which youth is worshiped and idolized by adults, in which young people are called "young adults," in which young people are portrayed in the media as wise, untainted gurus of insight, it's no wonder we convince young people that they're the hope of the world.

Funny…I thought Jesus was the hope of the world.

Modern youth ministry has turned discipleship into principles rather than a process, activity rather than inactivity. Discipleship has become a commitment that can be measured instead of a relationship that cannot be measured. Discipleship has become a short-term program instead of a lifetime process.

The church has decided to hurry young people into short-term results instead of taking the time to help them become intimate with the long-term Jesus.

Jesus' program of discipleship was simple: Hang out with the disciples; let them see you at your best and worst; spend lots of time alone; teach truths that none of your disciples can grasp at the moment; avoid crowds; go slowly; spend hours in solitude; don't worry about opposition; ignore criticism; don't expect immediate results.

Jesus knew hurried disciples become ex-disciples. Modern youth ministry needs to understand Jesus' mission:

Planting, watering, and waiting...in other words, unhurried discipleship.

Jesus knew, and so should we, that discipleship lasts a lifetime—not just in youth group.

May God help all of us to have ministries that *begin* discipleship.

THE "TROUBLE" WITH YOUTH MINISTRY
(MARCH 2001)

Youth ministry is dangerous. When you and I are trying to follow Jesus, we're going to get into trouble. Troublemaking is what discipleship looks like. Our role is not to create nice, compliant American citizens ready to get a good job and have 2.4 kids. Our job is to introduce young people to the life-ruining Jesus who causes nothing but trouble.

Listen...if your church doesn't have a rule that exists just because of your ministry (e.g., no soccer in the sanctuary, no orange punch in the fellowship hall), then you aren't letting Jesus have first place in your ministry. *Trouble* should be the youth worker's middle name.

Remember, all they can do is fire you.

A youth worker in our town was recently fired because he was reaching the "wrong kind of kid." I thought the wrong kind of kid was the right kind of kid.

The elders insisted that youth ministry wasn't about bringing in the "riffraff" off the streets but working with the kids who were already Christians.

I thought we were all riffraff.

A church in which the ethnic mix was changing hired a young woman to work with gang members. After a few weeks she gathered a few gang members for a Bible study. She actually talked them into coming to the church building for the study. One night she talked about Matthew 6:33 ("But seek first his kingdom and his righteousness...") and explained that if you want to be a disciple of Jesus, nothing can be more important than Jesus. Her words were, "If the gang is more important than Jesus, then the gang has to go. If your girlfriend is more important than Jesus, then she has to go."

One of the gang members was so into what she was saying that he threw his arms back and said, "Sh-t! It's hard to be a disciple!" Except when he swung his arms back, he broke a window that was set into the wall. The church leadership found out and was very upset at having to pay $26 to fix the window. They actually put the gang members on restriction and told them they couldn't meet in the church room for a week.

So I'm thinking to myself, *WHAT? WAS THIS CHURCH CRAZY?* Any leader who can teach the gospel so well that a group of gang members understands exactly what Jesus meant is one heck of a teacher! I want what she's got.

But it gets worse.

A few weeks later, the pastor accidentally interrupted one of the gang-member Bible studies. He sat down and spent a few minutes talking with the gang members. After he left, one of the guys said, "Hey, I like that guy. Let's go to church this Sunday." The youth worker decided to have the gang members sit in the balcony, rather than with the congregation downstairs. When the minister came out and announced the giving of the peace, one of the gang members stood up and yelled, "Hey, dude, you are cool!" The entire congregation turned around in shock. After the service the youth worker was told not to bring the gang members to church until they learned how to behave.

Again I'm thinking, *WHAT?* The entire congregation should have turned around, stood on their feet, and yelled back, "Hey, you guys are cool! Come on down here! You could really help us since none of us can see or hear!"

Then they should have given the youth worker a raise.

They didn't. She was fired.

Unfortunately, many people in the church are more concerned about rules, policies, and procedures than they are about the unbelievable, miraculous, spectacular, unprecedented, once-in-a-lifetime event that occurs when someone starts to get well. When people get well, it exposes the sickness of those around them.

Rather than getting mad, there should have been a celebration because a group of gang members miraculously desired to be part of the church.

Woo hoo!

Sometimes I wonder if it's easier for rocks to cry out in the presence of Jesus than for some church members to celebrate the "trouble" that genuine youth ministry causes.

SPEAKAHOLICS
(MAY 2001)

Hi. My name is Mike, and I am a speakaholic.

For most of my 40 years in ministry, I've found myself speaking a lot. I speak to young people, youth workers, churches, and numerous secular organizations. It all started very innocently. I had a gift of communication, I enjoyed using my gift, and others gave me the opportunity to use that gift.

Those opportunities increased every year, and eventually I was speaking in the morning, in the afternoon, and late at night. I even found myself sneaking in a speaking engagement right under my family's nose; I'd answer the phone and say, "yes," to speaking when my family had asked me to be home. But I couldn't stop.

Soon I became obsessed with speaking, and before I knew it, I'd graduated to *international speaking*. Not only was I gone much of the time, but when I was home, I was exhausted and no good to anyone around me because of jet lag and weariness. Before I knew what was happening, I was hopelessly addicted to communicating with others and was willing to sacrifice family, children, friends, and almost anything to have the opportunity to speak. Speaking was no longer what I did; it was who I was.

I am a speakaholic.

And guess what? Nobody cares.

People love speakaholics. There's a demand for speakers, an insatiable market for communicators; there are unlimited opportunities. It's not easy to communicate to this generation of adolescents, so those who can are in great demand for conferences, camps, retreats, and festivals. Speakers can quickly find themselves booked two or three years in advance.

I've met those who express a desire to develop a *speaking ministry*. Speaking is not a ministry; it's a narcotic, an addiction, a seduction stronger than sex. Speaking is tangled up in our egos, in control.

Speaking is dangerous.

Speaking creates an illusion of necessity, of power. Speakers are treated as special—just a notch above others. They're given honorariums, private housing, and all expenses paid.

Even within the niche world of the church, speakers develop a following, and they experience—in a small way—fame.

Fame is always dangerous. Fame is always destructive. Fame isolates speakers and convinces them that they're important—pivotal, even. Fame seduces speakers into believing their own press releases.

Speaking contaminates every speaker. And there are no exceptions. No speaker leaves the world of speakers unscathed. Not one. In fact, the only way a speaker can escape the negative consequences of speaking is to stop speaking.

There's no other way.

Speaking is a maximum-security prison from which there's no escape. Speaking is a drug much more dangerous than heroin because no one tries to stop you from your addiction; in fact, they encourage it. "I know you're busy, but is there any way you could squeeze us in?" "Hey, we don't want to take you away from your family so we'll pay for your family to come, too!"

And what about the side effects? Speakers live in abject terror of the day when no one invites them to speak anymore. Speakers complain and moan about their exhausting schedules while finding a way to squeeze in just one more speaking engagement. Speakers have no willpower, no discernment skills. They'll accept any and all invitations, no matter the price to them and to everyone around them.

So here's my solution.

Stop using speakers. Let's ban speakers from our youth groups, our camps, and our retreats. Let's boycott all speakers and let our love of young people do the speaking for us instead. Let's let our relationships do the talking.

And maybe, just maybe, we'll find a way to train young people to listen to the voice of Jesus speaking.

And to the speakers...we'll just say, "no."

If we don't, then we must bear some of the responsibility for the speakaholics we create. We must confess to our part in creating and encouraging speakaholics—in essence, becoming pimps of dependency.

We're the ones creating the demand, providing the drug, encouraging the addiction. We're the ones using speakers for our own ends without any consideration of the damage that speaking does to the speaker.

Just say "no."

We don't need speakers. We need listeners. We need more youth workers and more young people trained to listen to Jesus, to pay attention to what he's doing in the world, to notice where God is at work in their lives, and to hear "I love you" spoken by Jesus himself.

PILING ON THE MILLSTONES
(SEPTEMBER 2001)

Jesus said to his disciples, "Things that cause people to sin are bound to come, but woe to that person through whom they come. It would be better for him to be thrown into the sea with a millstone tied around his neck than for him to cause one of these little ones to sin. So watch yourselves." (Luke 17:1-3)

Nobody wants to say it, so I'll say it: Most adults in churches don't like kids.

That's why they hire youth workers—to keep the youth out of their hair. They're all in favor of youth Bible studies, youth group meetings, social events, and trips. Adults want youth group to be an activity center, an adolescent baby-sitting service. Parents want youth group to be the perfect alternative, a sanitized enhancement to the other important priorities of their children's lives—like hockey practice, ballet, SAT refresher courses, football camp, and, of course, studying. Youth group is the perfect place for young people when their schedules permit, and when nothing else more important is going on. Youth group is a great place to teach young people how to be good, upstanding citizens and future leaders in the business community—the ideal environment to teach young people how to be compliant, serious, and predictable.

Adults want young people to be conformed to the comfortable instead of transformed by the uncomfortable. Church is a great place, adults believe, to teach young people *about* Jesus.

But what about *encountering* Jesus?

Causing young people to meet Jesus face-to-face could do irreparable damage to parents' plans for their children. Introducing young people to the wild, untamed Jesus can cause havoc in a church that figured it had Jesus tamed. Meeting Jesus risks young people recognizing they're actually the church—the church *now*, not when they grow up.

Evil is most dangerous when it's subtle, when it's disguised in Christianity's clothing, when it baptizes secular values, when it snuffs out the light in young people's souls.

Tragically, many adults and churches are "causing...little ones who believe in Jesus to sin." Bring on the millstones.

We simply cannot allow youth ministry to become an extension of a soul-killing culture that's determined to seduce our children into being compliant, predictable, boring followers of Christ for whom discipleship has been reduced to watching the Power Team crunch blocks of ice.

No.

Youth group should be an adventure, a cauldron of fire and passion, an uncontainable and terrifying presence of the Holy Spirit overflowing into the souls of students and resulting in a volatile desire for Jesus, regardless of the chaos caused by following him.

Unfortunately, too many adults are more concerned about young people ruining the carpet than they are about Jesus ruining their lives. They're more upset by tattoos and earrings than the stress and busyness caused by parental expectations, more worried about peer pressure than parental pressure, more upset by unpredictability than predictability, and more fearful of the loss of future income than the loss of creativity and imagination.

More millstones, please.

May God give us a new generation of youth workers, unintimidated by denominations and institutions, who refuse to be held hostage to paychecks and who believe it's their calling to rescue this generation from the jaws of a comfortable, compliant, lifeless religion so they can proudly introduce this generation to the unstable, captivating, erratic, triumphant, upside-down, wondrous, inconsistent, irregular, noble, haphazard, awe-inspiring, stormy, magnificent, tempestuous, rowdy, dazzling, turbulent, outrageous, reckless, spectacularly glorious life of a disciple of Christ.

"I DON'T KNOW"
(NOVEMBER 2001)

Dear Youth Worker,

Please tell me why God allowed nearly 3,000 innocent people to be murdered on September 11, 2001?

Answer?

I don't know.

Where was God?

I don't know.

When Leslie Weatherhead, a minister in London during the Second World War, was asked by a member of his congregation where God was when his son was killed in a bombing raid, Weatherhead replied, "I guess He was where He was when His Son was killed."

And where was that?

I don't know.

Isn't "I don't know" too ambiguous? Isn't "I don't know" an unconvincing way to convince young people that Christianity is true?

Actually, "I don't know" confirms one critical truth about Christianity...it's a mystery.

Jesus loves us, right?

Of course.

So if he loves us, he protects us, right?

If he loves us...he is with us.

Jesus can heal, can't he? And perform miracles?

Of course. Just not very often.

Why?

I don't know.

What about God's will? My youth director says we're supposed to seek God's will. There are lots of verses in the Bible that tell us to do God's will, aren't there? God does have a will, right?

Absolutely.

Trouble is God's will is nothing like a to-do list. It's more like an undecipherable code. The Bible definitely gives us some clues about the code of God's will, which means we can figure out part of it; but, because it's from God, we'll never crack the code.

Clues?

Yeah. "Follow me...serve me...love me...live by my commandments...point people to me."

That's it? Just follow me, serve me, love me, obey me, and point people to me?

That's about it.

What do you mean "that's about it"?

You don't want to know.

Yes, I do.

We get a cross.

A cross?! What does that mean?

I don't know.

But God does heal people, right?

Certainly.

And miracles do happen, don't they?

Right.

So we can count on God helping us, can't we?

We can count on God being God.

Which means…?

I don't know.

And what does that mean?

It means we can trust God if we lost someone in the World Trade Center attacks, or if that person survived.

It means we can trust God when we have cancer, and when we're healed.

We can trust God if we survive a natural disaster, or if we don't.

We can trust God when we get a glimpse of divine will, and when we don't.

We can trust God in the answers and the questions, in the good and the bad, in the light and the dark, when we're winning, and when we're losing.

We can trust God even when the truth doesn't answer all of our questions or leaves us with even more questions.

And, most importantly, just beyond our "I don't knows," Jesus is waiting with open arms to snuggle us in the mystery of his love.

THE TRUTH SHALL MAKE YOU ODD
(JANUARY 2002)

What characterizes Christianity in the modern world is its oddness. Christianity is home for people who are out of step, unfashionable, unconventional, and counter-cultural. As Peter wrote, "strangers and aliens."

I pastor the slowest-growing church in America. We started 12 years ago with 90 members and have un-grown to 30. We're about as far as you can get from a user-friendly church—not because our congregation is unfriendly, but because our services are unpredictable, unpolished, and inconsistent.

We're an odd-friendly church, attracting unique and different followers of Christ who make every service a surprise. We refuse to edit oddness and incompetence from our services. We believe our oddness matters. We want our service filled with mistakes and surprises, because life is full of mistakes and surprises.

One Sunday morning, during the time for prayer requests, a member began describing the critical illness of her father. Because she was close to her father, her request for prayer was frequently interrupted by her own tears. Those around her reached out a hand or nodded with sadness. Some found their eyes filling with tears as well. The woman finished her request as best she could.

Seated in the front row was Sadie—a young woman with Down syndrome. Sadie stood and walked up the aisle until she saw the woman in the middle of her row. Stepping over the feet of other people in the aisle, Sadie reached the woman, bent down on her knees, laid her head on the woman's lap, and cried with her.

Sadie "inconvenienced" an entire row of people, stepped on their shoes, and forced them to make room for her… but none of us will ever forget that moment. Sadie is *still* teaching the rest of us what the odd compassion of Christ's church looks like.

Someone once said, "You shall know the truth, and the truth shall make you odd." Whoever made that statement understood what it means to be a follower of Christ. Followers of Christ are odd. Oddness is important because it's the quality that adds color, texture, variety, and beauty to the human condition. Christ doesn't make us the same. What he does is *affirm our different-ness.*

Oddness is important because the most dangerous word in Western culture is *sameness*. Sameness is a virus that infects members of industrialized nations and causes an allergic reaction to anyone who's different. This virus affects the decision-making parts of our brains, resulting in an obsession with making choices identical to those everyone else is making.

Sameness is a disease with disastrous consequences—differences are ignored, uniqueness is not listened to, gifts are canceled out, and the places where life, passion, and joy reside are snuffed out.

Sameness is the result of sin. Sin does much more than infect us with lust and greed; it flattens the human race, franchises us, and attempts to make us all homogenous. Sameness is the cemetery where our distinctiveness is dead. In a sea of sameness, no one has an identity.

But Christians do have an identity: Aliens! We're the odd ones, the strange ones, the misfits, the outsiders, the incompatibles. Oddness is a gift of God that sits dormant until God's Spirit gives it life and shape. Oddness is the consequence of following the One who made us unique, different...and *in his image!*

May our youth ministries be the homes of oddness, the places where different-ness is encouraged and sameness is considered sin, so the image of our holy and *odd* God will be lifted up for all to see.

YOUTH MINISTRY RANT
(MARCH 2002)

Ever have a bad day? Well, I'm having one, so I thought I might start ranting. Dennis Miller does it all the time on HBO, so why can't I? After 40-plus years in youth ministry, I'm ready to rant!

Is it just me, or are you also tired of seeing grown adults with their hats on backward?

Am I crazy, or does it bother anyone else that Christian music has an army full of pubescent, immature, dysfunctional little kids giving concerts and telling this generation of young people what Christianity is all about? Isn't it a bit weird to have a 14-year-old, spiked-haired misfit telling other 14-year-olds how to live life when they live it in a tour bus?

Does the world really need Christian T-shirts?

79

Can't we think of another word besides *extreme*?

I'm going to go crazy if I hear one more youth group chant-ing, "Gimme a J! Gimme an E...!"

What is it about the word *fire* that youth workers like so much?

Has anyone seen a tattoo that actually looks good?

Can someone please explain to me what breaking a stack of bricks with your head has to do with Jesus?

Can anyone explain Carman to me?

Can anyone explain Tulsa to me?

Can anyone explain *The Prayer of Jabez* musical to me?

What's with this new breed of youth workers who look like MTV clones but act like fundamentalists?

Remind me again why shaking the video camera while film-ing is cool?

Doesn't it bother anyone that so many older kids drop out of church, most of whom never return and abandon their faith, regardless of what techniques or programs we use?

What's the deal with Christian colleges anyway? Shouldn't they be graduating students who are revolutionary, anti-institutional, and anti-cultural? Isn't anyone else upset that most of our Christian colleges are graduating compliant, materialistic, irrelevant students who don't have a radical bone in their bodies? Who will push the envelope in the generations to come?

Why is it that youth groups never go to the opera, art museums, jazz festivals, ballet, modern dance recitals, poetry readings, professional theaters, or lectures?

Do we really believe it helps young people to tell them September 11 was actually the beginning of a revival?

Why does youth ministry worship thin, gorgeous, buff, cool, hot, sexy, beautiful people?

Explain to me what a "Christian Festival" is and why we need them?

Why would anyone who understands the gospel encourage young people to play sports in America?

Why would anyone who understands the gospel tell young people that God wants them to be winners, all-American, first, and top of the class?

Remind me again why we pray at football games. Does God really care who wins? Or loses?

Why are so many youth ministries concerned with putting on programs that no one remembers?

Why do so many youth ministries spend all their time talking about God instead of helping young people experience God?

Do youth ministers really believe that "big" (as in big youth groups, big events) matters to God?

Sometimes I worry that Jesus has left the youth ministry building…and no one's noticing.

Thank God that kids remember their relationships more than they remember programs.

Thank you, Jesus, that you've always worked through the small, the broken, and the powerless.

Thank you, God, that you find a way to chase young people into the kingdom in spite of all the frivolous programs, institutional obstacles, and silly youth ministry stuff that often chases young people away.

Thank you, Father, that you tolerate our egos, put up with our neediness, ignore our fascination with what doesn't matter, and still find ways to use us to draw young people into your presence.

Thank you, most of all, that you're a God who's big enough to ignore our rants.

TALKING DISCIPLESHIP
(MAY 2002)

Youth ministers talk too much. Most youth ministries are more like seminars than workshops, platforms than forums, lectures than discussions.

The result? Discipleship by talking. Youth ministry by indoctrination.

The model looks something like this:

> Tell them what to believe. Then tell them what to believe again. Then invite a guest speaker to tell them what to believe. (Or a musical group—most musical groups talk most of the time anyway. The difference is they sing first and *then* tell young people what to believe.)

What do we tell them to believe?

Read your Bible every day. Pray every day. Go to church often. Oh...and don't have sex.

Who decided that students reading their Bibles on a regular basis, praying, refraining from sexual activity, and going to church would result in dedicated, committed, long-term Christians? Who reduced the Christian faith to a to-do list?

I hate to say this—it sounds so obvious—but isn't the Christian life about our relationships with Jesus? Isn't youth ministry, then, about connecting young people to Jesus Christ? Experiencing Jesus Christ? Following Jesus Christ? Notice I didn't say *hearing about* Jesus, *talking about* Jesus, *cheering about* Jesus, *learning about* Jesus; I mean *being with* Jesus. Youth ministry is about young people being intimate with Jesus.

Uh oh. You mean youth ministry is not about connecting kids with the dazzling, good-looking, great-communicating, funny, athletic, charismatic youth leader? You mean reading the Bible every day, all day, doesn't guarantee a relationship with Jesus? Are you saying that if young people go to youth group every week, all year, they may never experience Jesus?

Yes, that's what I am saying.

Obviously, reading the Bible, praying, attending church, and not having sex can be part of one's relationship with Jesus; but I contend there's no direct correlation between those practices and intimacy, nor is there any guarantee of deepening discipleship when we engage in such practices. What's important is that young people seek the presence of Jesus in their lives, which almost always results from seeing this intimacy in others (i.e., their youth workers).

Look at the disciples. They spent all their time with Jesus. He did talk, but the disciples never understood a word he said. That didn't seem to bother Jesus, by the way. They saw Jesus in action, living his faith (healing, praying, losing his temper, agonizing, dying) and running from fame and power. They witnessed Jesus' relationship with his Father, which was turbulent to say the least—everything from gentle prayers to agonizing screams.

They watched Jesus taking time for himself, avoiding crowds, refusing to rush people into the kingdom. And they noticed that the majority of Jesus' time was spent with them. Oh, and one other thing: Jesus talked about all the issues facing the people of his time—all of them (the future, friendships, prayer, service, dealing with government, community, servanthood, humility, divorce, lust, poverty, the priority of following him over family, and so on).

What do we conclude? What's the job description of an effective youth minister? Effective youth ministers don't talk much; they spend enormous amounts of time with a few students, creating opportunities for students to experience God, to know God intimately, to be with God. They deal with the whole person, not just hormones (sex), egos (activities), and obvious problems (parents, school, drugs, alcohol). They also deal with kids' jealousy, insecurity, anger, depression, fear, doubt, guilt, restlessness, self-absorption, loss, confusion, and their concerns about justice, war, poverty, and reconciliation.

Above all, youth ministers have relationships with Jesus characterized by the absence of anxiety, the presence of humility, and a visible intimacy with him.

THE PROBLEM OF PARENTS
(JULY 2002)

What's the biggest obstacle to effective youth ministry? Parents.

Strange, isn't it? The people who most benefit from our ministry with their children are often the ones who create the most grief for our ministry.

Why are young people stressed out? Parents.

Why are young people obsessed with education, good grades, SAT scores, scholarships, college, college prep, pre-SATs? Parents.

Who encourages many of our youth to miss church, Bible study, camp, or service projects because of football camps, hockey practices, cheerleading clinics, gymnastics tournaments, and dance classes? Parents.

Who supports our ministries until their children have negative experiences or are disciplined or injured or don't like youth group or the music or their counselors or new sponsors or the way youth group is being run? Parents.

Who complains to the senior pastor, church board, session, deacons, and elders when something goes wrong (e.g., that old bus broke down, rain flooded the tents at a service project, someone got hurt, and so on) but never goes out of their way to affirm or encourage us when the ministry is going well? That would be parents.

Who automatically takes their children's side on any issue their sons or daughters are upset about? Parents.

Who has taught their sons and daughters that deadlines, rules, boundaries, and covenants are to be kept—unless they aren't kept, and then it's "not a big deal" or "too harsh" or "not clear" or "not fair" or "not understood" or "too strict" or "broken by everyone" or "should have been approved by the pastor"? Parents.

Who complains that the youth group has too many programs? Parents.

Who complains that the youth group doesn't have enough programs? The same parents who complain when their sons or daughters don't have enough to do.

Who never talks to their children about sex? Parents.

Who expects youth workers to talk to their children about sex? Parents.

Who complains that the youth worker's talk about sex was too explicit? The same parents.

Who never talks to their children about faith? Parents.

Who complains when their children aren't interested in faith? Parents.

Who's all in favor of their young people becoming serious about their faith, just as long as they don't take Jesus too seriously? Parents. Taking Jesus too seriously means altering parents' plans, vacation schedules, lifestyles—or worse, their dreams for their children.

So, Mike, you're anti-parent?

No.

Are you saying all parents are like this?

No, not all...just most.

So there are exceptions?

Certainly...but very few.

That's very pessimistic.

Yes, it is.

What about family ministry?

I'm all for it.

And...?

There just aren't very many families doing it...which is why youth ministry is so very important; but, to be honest, family ministry isn't biblical anyway.

WHAT?

Jesus told his disciples that he'd be the reason families break up.

Jesus said following him might cause a conflict between family loyalties and loyalty to him...and, when that happens, to choose him. Jesus is all for the family unless it gets in the way of following him.

Our job is not to make families better; our job is to encourage everyone in the family to take Jesus seriously, no matter the cost...even if that cost is family harmony.

No wonder parents are often the biggest obstacles to our ministries. No wonder our job security isn't all that great. No wonder youth ministry is a dangerous calling...and a rewarding one.

A BETTER IDEA THAN YOUTH MINISTRY
(SEPTEMBER 2002)

Youth ministry is a good idea. But there's a better idea.

Before we go there, let's look at what's good about the good idea of youth ministry.

GOOD YOUTH MINISTRY

RELEVANCE. Relevance is good. It means students can think, talk, write, and sing about the gospel in a language they not only understand, but also incorporate into their lives now. That's good. Very good.

RELATIONSHIPS. Relationships are good. Youth groups are places where kids can learn something about relationships, about friendships. They learn the value of praying together, working together, being together, and serving together. In healthy youth groups, they learn how to be less cruel toward those who are different; they're confronted with a gospel that asks us to love each other—even when the person to be loved is uncool, ugly, uncoordinated, overweight, or a geek. That is good. Very good.

SAFETY. Safety is good. It gives young people a glimpse of grace. At its best, youth ministry is a place where students are safe: Safe to be honest, to be real, and to express what's deep in their souls. Not all youth groups are safe; but where there is safety, it is good. Very good.

FUN. Fun is good, too. Very good. Young people have very few places where they're encouraged to have fun. Students should spend a lot of their childhood laughing. Youth ministry helps young people rediscover genuine laughter and fun. Fun is good. Very good.

Youth group is good.

But there's a better good.

It's called *church*.

CHURCH

Not youth church, or contemporary church, or postmodern church. Just plain, boring, ordinary church. Yes, that's right. Church. The place where people who don't know each other get to know each other; where people who normally don't associate with each other, associate; where people who are different from each other learn how to be one.

Mostly, church is the place where we can grow old together. And it turns out that growing old together is still the best way to bring lasting results with students. Growing old together is where we teach (and learn from) each other what discipleship means in the everyday world.

I pastor a church that for the last 16 years hasn't had a youth program (in spite of the fact that I can provide free resources). Nothing. Just church on Sunday mornings at 10 o'clock, where students have to muddle through a very uncool service filled with mistakes, awkward gaps, interruptions, and imperfections. The music? In the language of students...it "sucks." We've never had many students at our services, but we've always had some.

And here's the crazy part: The few students we've had over the years? They keep coming back. Most of our students leave town for college or work; but when they're back in town, they're back in church, usually fighting back the tears. Why?

"It feels like home," they say. "Everyone's so glad to see me. After all these years, I still feel like I belong here. It's like Jesus never left the building."

Somehow, being with a group of diverse people week after week caused a bond to form—a family was created and community happened. The mystery of community became a reality. Community isn't complicated. It's just a group of people who grow old together. They stick with each other through the teenage years, marriage, children, getting old, getting sick, and finally dying—all the while teaching each other how to follow Christ through the rugged terrain of life.

Maybe the body of Christ is where youth ministry was supposed to happen all along.

One of my sons lives near San Francisco. He still considers our church his home church. I asked him why. "Stuart Higgs," he replied without hesitation. Stuart is in his 60s, slowing, succumbing to the ravages of MS, divorced, and still clinging to Jesus. During the years when his life was turned upside down by what I've just described, Stuart managed to find the time to love my son, seek him out after church, pray for him, stay connected to him, and, in the process, mentor and disciple him. Stuart Higgs may not fit the profile of the hip, postmodern youth worker, but he was my son's youth worker.

The morning services at Grace Church are a long way from "exciting youth programs," but it's the only youth ministry we have. I wonder what would happen if churches truly decided to take responsibility for their young people? They could still have youth programs and youth workers, but the real youth ministry would happen when all the adults decided to connect with all the kids and do church together. Maybe there would be fewer students coming to church than attending youth group; but a decade later, the ones who connected at church might still be there.

GETTING FIRED FOR THE GLORY OF GOD
(NOVEMBER 2002)

After spending time with youth workers from all over the world during Youth Specialties' National Youth Workers Convention, there's no question in my mind that our calling to youth ministry and the condition of the institutional church are on a collision course.

I'm beginning to believe that if those called to youth ministry follow the lead of the One who called them, then getting fired is inevitable.

Why? Because, in general, the institutional church doesn't get it. The institutional church has become hopelessly corporate, hopelessly tangled in a web of secularism. Instead of the church being *the church*, it has opted to be a corporation.

You disagree? Why don't you try these seven suggestions, and see how long you keep your job?

1. KEEP JESUS #1. Make your relationship with Jesus the first priority in your life and expect the same from your church staff. Suggest that staff meetings allow only discussion about everyone's relationship with Jesus. Forget about business; just pray together and share your struggles with each other.

2. BE STILL. Require as part of your job description paid time alone with God. At least one day a week of silence, three-day retreats every quarter, and one week a year for the entire staff.

3. IGNORE CORPORATE VALUES. Refuse to accept corporate values for evaluating your worth. And what are those corporate, secular, humanist values?

- Size
- Productivity
- Efficiency
- Speed
- Technology
- Busyness
- Measuring
- Balance
- Power

- Success

- Good grades

- Sports

Instead...

4. *THINK SMALL.* Keep your youth group small and manageable. Work hard to focus on a few rather than many. Don't let your group get larger than you can handle with integrity.

5. *BE REAL.* Tell the truth. Tell students when you're doubting, struggling, hurting, and failing. Create an atmosphere of reality. Refuse to edit your meetings so only the polished communicators speak and only the positive stories get told.

6. *PUT YOUR FAMILY FIRST.* Don't let a workaholic staff intimidate you into becoming a workaholic, too. Say "yes" to your family first.

7. *SEEK KINGDOM VALUES.* What are kingdom values?

- *Time.* Have plenty of extra time to spend with students—one-on-one. Refuse to be too busy.

- *Awareness.* Sensitivity, empathy, noticing.

- *Audacity.* Risk, courage, resistance.

- *Intimacy with God.*

- *Humility.*

- *Grace.*

Notice: You don't have to confront the system. You can just get close to Jesus, seek intimacy with God, follow kingdom values…and it won't be long until you're out on the street.

And guess who will be there with you?

You got it…Jesus.

YOU JUST HANG ON
(JANUARY 2003)

I don't know why volunteers volunteer.

I don't understand why most professional youth workers decide to stay in ministry. Most of you are underpaid, unappreciated, disrespected, mistreated, and abandoned.

Oh, I know there are exceptions. There's a small minority of youth workers paid adequately and treated well, but the rest—the majority—are beaten down, burned out, and constantly criticized.

We just finished our three National Youth Worker Conventions, and I was once again made painfully aware of how badly most youth workers are treated by the churches they serve.

ALL ABOUT NUMBERS

One youth worker told me his job is now in jeopardy because his senior pastor recently went to a megachurch seminar and decided they're now going to become a megachurch, too. The pastor returned and announced, "You need to get with the program or think about going somewhere else. Your youth group is way too small, so you need to step up to the plate."

Now here's the crazy truth: In the majority of churches, if your youth group numbers run around 10 percent of the total congregation, you're normal. Ten thousand in your church? One thousand kids. One hundred in your congregation? Ten kids. It really doesn't matter if you're Ed Schmuck or Doug Fields; 10 percent ain't bad.

Sadly, for many churches it's all about numbers, and the youth workers in these churches end up judging their own worth and ministries by how many kids attend their events. Lots of kids? You're doing a great job. Few kids? You're worthless.

But for many youth workers, the lack of numbers isn't killing you—it's the constant criticism that eats at your soul and makes you wonder why you're doing this.

CONSTANT CRITICISMS

YOU'RE BRINGING IN THE WRONG KIDS. "You were hired to minister to the children of our church, not to bring in 'riffraff' from the outside. Those kids could have a negative

YOU JUST HANG ON

influence on the good kids we have." Hmmm. I thought the wrong kids were the right kids. I didn't realize youth workers were hired to baby-sit the church kids so Mom and Dad could have some time to themselves.

THE KIDS MISBEHAVE. "They're too loud (so is their music), they don't sit still in church, or they don't even bother to come. They're rude, and they often interrupt or ask disruptive questions. And they dress weird. Can't you talk to them about the way they dress—especially for church?"

YOU HAVE TOO MANY PROGRAMS. Oh, they want you to have lots of options, lots of things for the kids to do, as long as they don't interfere with sports, drama, ballet, SATs, college visits, and so on. Any time there's a conflict between church camp and football camp, you're supposed to understand which is more important...and it isn't church camp. When one youth worker suggested that spending a weekend thinking about God was more important than the regional finals in swimming, she was told she needed to get her priorities straight.

THE YOUTH DON'T RESPECT PROPERTY. How many times do you get in trouble because of a stain on the carpet, a mark on the wall, trash in the parking lot, or cigarette butts in the Jones Memorial Rose Garden? Or because kids are sitting on the "holy" furniture, lying on the floor, or leaning against the wall? I'm sorry, but I thought the building was meant for actual use. I thought stains, marks, and kids all over the place were good things. I didn't realize that protecting the building was more important than using it.

THE KIDS ARE DANGEROUS. "Why, I was almost knocked over by a skateboarder! Can't you do something about them?" Yeah, I guess you should tell the skater kids not to come so the churchy folks will feel more comfortable. Bummer, too, because I thought the fact that skateboarders even want to be at our church is cause for celebration—not a nuisance to be eliminated.

YOU MAKE MISTAKES. Duh. Of course you make mistakes. That's what happens when you follow Jesus with passion. Mistakes are part of success. Mistakes validate your ministry because it means you're taking risks.

No wonder so many youth workers call it quits. No wonder volunteers decide to un-volunteer. What's a wonder is how many youth workers decide to stick it out. You keep going even when your budgets are cut, your salaries are lowered, and your integrity is questioned. Your lives have been ruined by your callings. What can you do? You just hang on because…well…because Jesus hung on (if you know what I mean).

I'm in awe of youth workers, and I think Jesus is, too. I just wish the church felt the same way.

HOW PASTORS CAN KEEP YOUTH WORKERS
(MARCH 2003)

I have a solution for the long-held belief that youth workers average about 18 months in a church before they move on or are moved out. I guarantee that if pastors implement my suggestions, then the average stay of a youth worker could triple or even quadruple. We're talking "miracle" here.

1. Believe that your primary job as pastor is to care for the spiritual life of your youth worker. Support your youth worker at any cost because it will cost you.

2. Explain to the church that you expect the youth worker to be "out of the office" most of the time because a youth worker's office is the car, McDonald's, football stands, band hall, and surfboard.

3. Remind the church that when your youth worker's at camp, she's working.

4. When your youth worker makes a mistake, come to his defense. Help the church understand that mistakes are part of the job and that you couldn't be more pleased that you have a youth worker who's taking risks and pushing the envelope.

5. Keep pushing to increase the youth worker's salary and the youth budget.

6. Once a year, encourage church members with the means to provide a weekend getaway at a cabin or beach house or condo for the youth worker and her family. Stock the refrigerator with food, arrange for baby-sitting, and tell her to take the weekend off— she deserves it.

7. Support his family. Encourage your youth worker to divide the day into three parts and work only two of them. Check on his marriage and give him plenty of slack when the new baby arrives.

8. Before the job even starts, meet with the youth worker and then the board to make sure everyone's on the same page when it comes to expectations and results. Whatever you do, make sure that numbers and attendance aren't the sole or even primary success markers.

9. Now that you've hired a youth worker, don't expect that she'll do all the youth work. Expect the congregation to volunteer, and if there's no response, go with the youth worker to personally invite others to help. Believe that for every five kids in the middle or high school youth group, there should be one adult volunteer spending time with those kids on a regular basis.

10. Include young people in the life of the church, not just youth night. In fact, don't have youth night. Put teenagers on boards, have them participate in the services and as greeters, and encourage the senior members of the congregation to "adopt" kids in the youth group so each has an older mentor, friend, pen pal, and wise sage. Encourage both the kids and the seniors to exchange letters and tiny gifts for birthdays and special moments, and have the students put on a dinner once a year for their older pals.

11. Spend a lot of your time working with parents, providing them with resources and seminars ("Understanding Your Teenager," for instance) to help families sift through what's important during the critical teenage years.

12. Part of the youth worker's job description should be the expectation that she takes one day a week, three days every three months, and one week a year just for working on her soul. Also give her a budget for books that are just about the care of the soul.

13. Meet with youth on a regular basis and have open question-and-answer sessions so they can get to know you as a person. Let them know your struggles, your flaws, and your passion for them.

14. Ask the wisest elder in your church to attend the youth group meetings and report back each month what he observed.

15. Plan service projects designed for youth and adults to work together.

16. Continually affirm and encourage your youth worker.

There you have it. A happy youth worker is a long-term youth worker. Woo hoo!

THE FAILURE OF YOUTH MINISTRY
(MAY 2003)

What's the most important function of youth ministry?

    A. Introducing young people to Jesus

    B. Providing healthy activities

    C. Involving young people in service

    D. Writing abstinence pledges

    E. Offering good theological training

    F. Leading worship

Answer: None of the above.

The most important function of youth ministry is longevity. Long-term discipleship.

It's my contention that the vast majority of youth ministries focus all of their time and energy on the "none of the aboves" and very little on longevity. How do I know?

LOOK AT THE RESULTS

Attend any youth group in this country, and you'll notice the "aging effect." Attendance is directly proportional to age: The older the students, the fewer who are likely to attend youth group. Typically there are more freshmen than sophomores, more sophomores than juniors, and more juniors than seniors.

I'm sure there are many reasons for this phenomenon. Older students are more likely to work, more likely to drive, and more likely to be extremely busy. But the real reason is that older students are much more likely to lose interest in Christianity, lose the desire to stay close to Christ, or lose the willingness to pay the price of commitment. In the everyday battle for the souls of older students, the lure of the secular is just too strong.

Almost every study out there shows that when it comes to moral behavior, there's no difference between non-Christian and Christian students. They drink as much, screw as much, have oral sex as much, and party as much.

Why?

YOUTH MINISTRY DOESN'T HAVE ANY STAYING POWER

Young people flock to Christian concerts, cheer Jesus at large events, and work on service projects. Unfortunately, it's not because of Jesus; it's because they're young.

The success of youth ministry in the United States is an illusion.

Very few youth ministries have a lasting impact on students.

I believe we're no more effective today at reaching young people with the gospel than we've ever been. In spite of all the dazzling youth ministry superstars, the amazing array of Youth Specialties products, and the thousands of youth ministry training events, nothing much has changed.

FOLLOWING JESUS IS HARD

Faith is difficult. Discipleship requires a huge investment of time. And most of us don't have the time. Or we choose not to take the time. Or our current models of ministry don't allow us the time.

SO LET'S BE HONEST

Youth ministry as an experiment has failed. If we want to see the church survive, then we need to rethink youth ministry.

What does that mean? I don't have a clue. But my hunch is that if we want to see young people have a lasting faith, then we have to completely change the way we do youth ministry in America.

I wonder if any of us has the courage to try.

AN APOLOGY
(JULY 2003)

I have an apology to make.

In my rush to make deadline, my previous column communicated the wrong message.

What I thought I said and what many people read were two quite different things.

I was hoping to throw some cold water on the high-profile ministries that give the impression they're attracting gazillions of young people to their ministries and changing the lives of gazillions more.

I was trying to level the playing field by introducing a dose of reality.

My hope was that the person in Podunk, Iowa, would be encouraged. My hope was that the majority of us who have smaller ministries would realize that no matter how much press a particular ministry gets, the results are the same for all of us. Besides, according to Jesus and his parable of the seed, the best we can hope for is about 25 percent.

At least one reader, Ken McDonald, a volunteer youth worker from Texas, heard me:

> I've been a volunteer youth worker pushing 10 years. I eat lunch with the students every day. I go to their ballgames and soccer matches. I've been to countless funerals for their grandparents, parents, and friends. I spend hours each week talking to them online. I'm an elder, and I've tried to incorporate them into the life of the church. I pray for them, send them birthday cards, and take them sailing to scare the hell out of them. But this year, the students I've spent the most time with, prayed the hardest for, and lost the most sleep over are seniors. In a few months they'll be gone.
>
> Taking stock, of the five to 10 closest students, only one of them is regularly in church or youth group. The others got their driver licenses and never came back or just faded into oblivion. And they were students who wrote passionate poems about Jesus and his love, cluttered up AOL's trunk lines with hundreds of forwards saying, "If you love Jesus, you'll pass this on," built porches on mobile homes in Appalachia, worshiped at "Fun in the Son," rang handbells on Sundays, and crawled under flooded homes to install insulation. But one by one they disappeared.

Ken understood my point. All the hype about youth ministry simply hides the painful reality that no matter what we do, most of the kids we work with "disappear."

But what most of you read was, "Youth ministry is worthless, useless, and not worth doing." I apologize. The last thing I want to do is discourage youth workers.

What I intended (and didn't accomplish) was to un-intimidate youth workers who are discouraged by all of the "successful" ministries that claim results that are different from the rest of ours.

Luckily, like most of you, Ken McDonald understands youth ministry. And, like you, he's the real deal. He concludes his letter:

> So it feels like it's time to throw in the towel. Pull off the river, dump out the raft, and head for home. Take up gardening and try nurturing plants for a while instead of young people.
>
> There's just one problem. God won't let me do it.
>
> The call remains.
>
> The bat-infested, apathetic place I call church is my lot at the moment. Those seniors are my seniors, and God has placed us together for some weird reason.

Maybe the institution of youth ministry is a failure, but it hasn't failed all young people.

Maybe techniques and programs don't work very well, but they work for some.

Maybe many of the young people we work with don't make it, but some do.

Maybe our programs aren't effective for all, but they're effective for some.

Maybe our programs aren't changing the world, but they're changing some.

Maybe most kids disappear, but not all of them do.

Maybe we don't need a revolution in youth ministry; maybe what we need is what we've always needed—a few adults willing to follow God's call to love young people into the kingdom of God no matter what the result...like Ken McDonald...and like you.

DISCIPLE ABUSE
(SEPTEMBER 2003)

Suppose I took a group of dedicated high school football players and said to them, "If you're really committed, if you're serious about football, if you genuinely want to be the best, then I'm taking you to an NFL training camp so you can be professional football players."

You'd look at me like I was crazy. These young people, passionate and dedicated as they are, would be slaughtered on that football field. They'd be destroyed physically and mentally. And I, as a coach, would be arrested for child abuse.

Then why do we say to junior high and high school students who sincerely want to follow Jesus and give their lives to God, "You need discipleship class. If you're really committed and dedicated, then attend a discipleship class where you can become even more dedicated and committed. We're going to make you a disciple"? If we do this, then we're guilty of disciple abuse.

I don't believe in student discipleship.

I believe in encouragement, affirmation, education, service, and study. I believe in relationship, community, and fellowship. I believe in training, beginning, starting, and learning. I believe in praying together, playing together, talking together, hanging out together, and living life together. But I don't believe in "pouring my life into students." I believe in showing my life to students and living my life in front of students, but I don't believe in discipling young people.

"TOO...YOUNG"

Young people are too...well...young to be disciples.

Apprentices? Of course. Beginners? Sure. Trainees? Interns? Absolutely. But not disciples.

We've convinced adults and parents that we have programs that can produce disciples. We perpetuate the illusion that we can take 13-year-olds and make disciples out of them. We actually act as though we can transform a group of inconsistent, uncommitted adolescents into mature, committed disciples by spending an extra hour or two a week with them.

Not possible.

Are students capable of heroic acts? Absolutely! Can a 13-year-old be committed to Jesus? Yes...as long as we understand what we mean by "committed." Can young people make a difference in the world? Of course they can, but we're still not talking about disciples.

"DISCIPLESHIP REQUIRES..."

Discipleship isn't about coming to more meetings than non-disciples. It's not about leadership or getting involved in service projects. Discipleship isn't about filling out a book-let. It's a way of living; it's the process of figuring out what it means to believe in Jesus in the everydayness of life.

Because most students in our youth groups have been pro-tected from suffering. (Remember all those parents who showed up for your Mexico orientation, concerned about the safety of the trip? And you lied and said it would be safe?) Because Mom and Dad have continually rescued most students, and because most students haven't been prepared for the real world, they're not prepared for the complicatedness of life.

Discipleship requires maturity, experience, and depth. Discipleship requires extensive time. Discipleship requires intensity, isolation, and independence. Discipleship requires spending time with Jesus—not with you and me. Disciple-ship requires a lifetime of figuring out what it means to follow Jesus.

"RUIN THEIR LIVES..."

Before the mail starts pouring in, by all means, spend time with young people, study with them, pray with them, introduce them to Jesus, affirm them, encourage them, challenge them, attract them, motivate them, suffer with them, cry with them, and push them. Ruin their lives by introducing them to the compelling, attractive, demanding, frightening Jesus.

Most of all, love them. Believe in them. Trust them. Be an example for them. Stick it out with them over the long haul. And some day, when they're older, when they've weathered a few storms, when they've been beaten up by life a bit, they may actually start looking like a disciple—not because you discipled them, but because you refused to give up on them.

CARING FOR YOUR OWN SOUL WHILE MINISTERING TO OTHERS

Everyone was saying that I was doing really well,
but something inside was telling me
that my success was putting my own soul in danger.

—Henri Nouwen, *In the Name of Jesus*

The call of God is difficult to explain but impossible to ignore. It's the nagging, conscious awareness asking you to do something. The asking comes not from words, but from deep within, as though a voice had been planted inside and now is beginning to speak. This voice, the calling voice, has many ways of speaking—your passion for young people, the unique parts of you that seem to attract young people, the sense of joy and fulfillment that overflows into your soul when you're with young people. It's the great YES of your life that fills you with a sense of belonging, the warmth of being home.

Heady wine, this call to youth ministry.

The call of youth ministry is unmistakable, relentless, captivating. And dangerous. Because, in reality, it's a job. And once ministry becomes a job, the rules all change and Youth Ministry the Job conflicts with Youth Ministry the Call.

Youth Ministry the Job has job descriptions, performance objectives, mission statements, evaluation forms. It's about measuring—how many, how much...growth, success, results. Youth Ministry the Call, on the other hand, is a mystery—and (trust me) the mystery of youth ministry is very frustrating for church boards and executive pastors.

Youth Ministry the Call has a rhythm all its own—slow.

- Youth Ministry the Job is about wider. Youth Ministry the Call is about deeper.
- Youth Ministry the Job is about more. Youth Ministry the Call is about one.
- Youth Ministry the Job is about program. Youth Ministry the Call is about relationship.
- Youth Ministry the Job is about being in your office. Youth Ministry the Call is being wherever young people hang out.
- Youth Ministry the Job is about young people's souls. Youth Ministry the Call is about your soul.

In my first years of youth ministry, my reckless passion for young people, my burning desire to introduce young people to Jesus, and my ego and arrogance had a kind of momentum. It was the late '60s, and the world was ready to bless anyone willing to help America's wayward and rebellious youth. I was anxious to get started, and my church was anxious for me to get started. It never occurred to my church or to me that something critical was being ignored—my soul.

Not much has changed. The urgency of young people's needs combined with the demands of programs and expectations—these push youth ministers along at ever increasing speeds. As long as young people are showing up and parents are happy, no one—least of all the youth minister—is inclined to ask, "What price is being paid to keep this program moving at such a fast pace?"

The road I've traveled for the last 40 years is lined with the burned-out remains of youth workers who discovered too late the need to care for their own souls. "Hey, my passion for God will never diminish," you say. "I'll never allow myself to reach the place where my soul is in danger." I hope you're right. But my experience tells me our souls are especially in danger when we're in youth ministry. Youth ministry is a seduction. Once you've experienced how young people respond to you, listen to you, and want to be like you—these things make it very difficult to think about your soul. The instant gratification of relationships with young people drowns out the delayed gratification of a relationship with Jesus.

I wish someone had warned me about the hazards of youth ministry. I wish someone had sat me down and told me what they wished they'd known when they started out in youth ministry. I wish someone had flagged me down while I was rushing around fulfilling everyone's expectations. (Of course, maybe they did, but I was going too fast to see them.) So I feel obliged to share what I've learned from my mistakes and warn youth workers of the obstacles ahead. I mean, it took me 50 years to understand what intimacy with Jesus even meant. To the contrary, I spent most of my youth ministry years trying to prove to Jesus that I was worthy of his love by trying to impress him with all I was doing.

In *Stories Jesus Still Tells*, John Claypool writes about trying to put his four-year-old to bed while she took three trips to the bathroom, asked for a drink of water, wanted another story told, needed Dad to put the light on, heard sounds, and so on. When she finally settled down, John retreated upstairs to write. He was deep into his writing when he sensed his daughter standing at the study door. He turned around. "Laura, what do you want me to do?" he asked with more irritation in his voice than he wanted to betray. She padded into the room and grabbed his arm. "Nothing, Daddy. I just want to be close to you."

I was too long in youth ministry before I let myself hear Jesus whispering to me, "I don't want you to do anything right this minute—I just want to be close to you." I might have learned this a lot earlier if someone had told me then what I want to tell you now:

YOU ARE RESPONSIBLE FOR YOUR OWN RELATIONSHIP WITH GOD

When I signed on at my first church, I looked forward to spending many hours with my new boss, talking about our faith. I looked forward to being mentored by this godly man I admired. He was seminary trained; I was not. He had lived many years; I was very young. In fact, a big reason I took this job was because of the opportunity to learn from the wisdom of this pastor. Talk about disillusionment. I never saw him. We hardly conversed; when we did, it was about some youth activity or an upcoming mission trip or the lock-in the next week. My pastor was distant, preoccupied, and seldom talked about his own relationship with Jesus.

Then there were staff meetings. After a string of "regular" jobs during college, I was eager to be among staff who talked about Jesus during their meetings. Talk about disappointment. Each meeting began with prayer, but the remainder was all about the choir, the carpet, the building campaign, Vacation Bible School, the parking lot, the budget, and the damage to Fellowship Hall after the latest lock-in. Seldom did we talk about the Bible or our relationships with Jesus. Even our prayers were typically about church business—at best they were about church members who were sick or in need. I had unconsciously counted on my pastor and staff to help me stay on track with Jesus. I expected the business of the church to be incidental to the Jesus of the church. I couldn't have been more wrong.

Though it may sound harsh, this was the truth: It took me a long time to realize that no one cared about my relationship with Jesus. Oh, they cared plenty if my dry soul caused me to run off with the organist. But when it came to routine business and weekly meetings, no one expressed any interest in my relationship with Jesus. My relationship with Jesus was assumed. It was up to me to keep current with Jesus. It was up to me to find time in my busy schedule to find time for God. It was up to me to struggle with my own faith. The institution simply expected me to come to work every day with my faith intact. Yes, our conversations carried the appropriate God-talk. Yes, we often prayed about specific issues that had arisen in our church. Yes, we even talked about the Bible once in a while. But it was clear that we were hired to do the work of the church. The work of the soul was to be done after hours, on my own time.

Which is actually good news, of course, because we are responsible for our own spiritual nurture and growth. If you want to survive spiritually, then take charge of your own relationship with Christ—perhaps along these lines:

- *WRITE INTO YOUR JOB DESCRIPTION: TIME ALONE WITH JESUS.* Ask for a day each week or a weekend each month or a week every six months to work on your soul. These days can be spent in solitude, silence, on spiritual retreat, or prayer retreat—whatever it takes to listen for God in your life.

- *ASK FOR A BOOK BUDGET THAT'S SEPARATE FROM YOUR YOUTH MINISTRY BOOK BUDGET.* Ask for money to buy books about the spiritual life—just for you, not to create lessons for your students.

• *SUGGEST THAT THE STAFF GET TOGETHER WEEKLY OR EVEN DAILY FOR COMMUNION (THAT WOULD BE EUCHARIST) TO HELP EVERYBODY REMEMBER THEIR CALLING.*

• *FIND A WISE, OLDER PERSON WHO'LL AGREE TO MEET WITH YOU REGULARLY TO HELP YOU LISTEN TO WHAT GOD IS SAYING IN YOUR LIFE.* (That would be a spiritual director.)

• *JOURNAL REGULARLY.* Journaling gets you in touch with your interior. Your writing often reveals a part of you that you weren't consciously paying attention to.

• *ASK THE STAFF TO BRAINSTORM WAYS TO INCREASE THE PERCENTAGE OF TIME DURING STAFF MEETINGS SPENT TALKING ABOUT THEIR RELATIONSHIPS WITH JESUS.* (There will always be business to discuss, so be realistic.) If the staff now spends 90 percent of the time talking about business and 10 percent about their souls, see if you can get them to agree to 80/20; then later maybe even 70/30.

• *SUGGEST THAT THE STAFF HAVE ANNUAL (OR SEMI-ANNUAL OR MONTHLY) SPIRITUAL RETREATS.* The only activity on the schedule is everybody caring for their own relationships with God.

YOU ARE MORE IMPORTANT THAN YOUR STUDENTS

Sounds selfish, I know. "Seek ye first the kingdom of God," you remind me. Yet you'll tend to spend all your energy on your students' spiritual lives. If you're like most youth workers, then you'll gradually wear down to the point of reading the Bible primarily for ideas for your talks and lessons rather than for your own relationship with God. If you're like most youth workers, then your praying will tend to occur only during meetings or church events. Before you know it, you're living your spiritual life vicariously through others: You'll hear a sermon or read a good book and you'll think only what a good talk illustration it'll make. When a teenager in your group makes a life-changing decision, that moment becomes a prop for your spirituality—rather than you relying on your own decisions and your own life-changing moments.

If you want to avoid this terribly easy slide from Youth Ministry the Call to Youth Ministry the Job, then you'll have to remember we're not about fixing people or situations. We're about being with Jesus. The best gift you can give a young person is not to fix their problems but to help them recognize the presence of a Jesus who will never leave them nor forsake them, even when their lives plod along unfixed.

When young people observe the unfixed, broken you and your relationship with God, they learn the power of their own relationships with God in the middle of their brokenness. If your youth ministry begins with your relationship with Jesus instead of theirs, then working on your own soul isn't periphery or extracurricular—it's central to your ministry. Your soul is your ministry.

Real ministry is not what you do, but who you are.

DON'T SPIRITUALIZE SPIRITUALITY

Taking care of your soul doesn't mean retiring to a monastery. Once I guiltily confessed to my friend, Brennan Manning, my embarrassment at how comparatively little effort I'd made at taking the time to be alone with God when during the previous year he'd done numerous silent retreats (for varying durations—weekends, one week, 30 days). "Mike, quit being so hard on yourself," he told me. "You think about God all the time. That is prayer. Even now you are praying all day long. Just because I'm on a 30-day silent retreat doesn't mean I'm on my knees praying the whole time—I'm reading, walking, sleeping, watching birds, thinking about my next speaking engagement."

I didn't recognize my own relationship with God because I'd put Brennan on a pedestal. I compared my life to his. And consequently, prayer became inaccessible to me. Whenever you compare what you don't know about someone else to everything you know about you, you lose. I couldn't be Brennan Manning, and I don't have to be. I still haven't been on a seven-day silent retreat. But what I have done over the years is find my own way of being with God. Granted, my relationship with Jesus is erratic and irregular. I have periods of time where I read voraciously, pray a lot, and spend much time thinking about my Savior. Then there are dry, barren times when I wonder where God is. My irregular schedule has become a regular part of my life, and it works for me. I don't have a routine for my prayer life. I don't have routines for any part of my life. I'm not a routine kind of guy. What's important is to understand what kind of man or woman you are—and then be true to that person in your walk with God.

READ LIKE A MANIAC

Most youth workers don't read nearly enough. Yet reading is absolutely essential to your spiritual growth.

• *ASK THE PEOPLE WHOM YOU ADMIRE AND RESPECT WHAT BOOKS THEY READ.* If you're drawn to certain people, then chances are they have the same reading interests you do—so trust them to get you on the right track.

• *NOTE THOSE AUTHORS YOU RESONATE WITH, THEN GET ALL OF THEIR BOOKS.* (I have my own group of authors who, through their books, have become my reading-world friends: Eugene Peterson, Barbara Brown Taylor, Walter Wangerin Jr., John Claypool, Earl Palmer, Henri Nouwen, Calvin Miller, Frederick Buechner, Alan Jones, Will Willimon, Evelyn Underhill, and Philip Yancey. I read everything they write. Somehow they know me; they name my struggles and put into words what I've been unable to find words for.)

• *PLACE THOSE FEW BOOKS THAT HAVE REALLY AFFECTED YOU IN A BOOKCASE CLOSE TO WHERE YOU WORK.* In my study I have all my favorite books—my friends—just to the left of my desk and within arm's reach. I have lots more books in my study, but my friends are right next to me.

• *INTERACT WITH YOUR BOOKS.* Mark your favorite passages, make notes, mark and then file the quotes that grip you. Books are made to be marked—and stained with tears, too. Reading is more than gathering information—it's a relationship.

• *DON'T WORRY IF YOU TAKE A BREAK FROM READING NOW AND THEN.* Sometimes your soul needs space and time to process what's going on in your life. At such times reading can distract you from the soul work you should be doing.

• *WHATEVER YOU DO, DON'T LIMIT YOUR READING TO SPIRITUAL BOOKS.* Read recent novels, old classics, biographies, short stories, essays, articles. Christians aren't the only ones speaking truth. Truth is truth, regardless of who says it.

For what it's worth, the following is my recommended reading list. Let it start you on the path to making your own book list:

Bob Benson Sr. and Michael W. Benson, *Disciplines for the Inner Life* (Word)

Robert Benson, *Between the Dreaming and the Coming True: The Road Home to God* (HarperSanFrancisco)

Walter Brueggemann, *The Prophetic Imagination* (Fortress)

Thomas Cahill, *The Gifts of the Jews: How a Tribe of Desert Nomads Changed the Way Everyone Thinks and Feels* (Nan A. Talese/Anchor Books)

Christopher de Vinck, *The Power of the Powerless: A Brother's Legacy of Love* (Zondervan)

Jacques Ellul, *The Presence of the Kingdom* (Seabury)

Suzanne G. Farnham and others, *Listening Hearts: Discerning Call in Community* (Morehouse)

Arthur Gordon, *A Touch of Wonder: Staying in Love with Life* (Jove Books)

Thelma Hall, *Too Deep for Words: Rediscovering Lectio Divina* (Paulist)

Abraham J. Heschel, *Man's Quest for God: Studies in Prayer and Symbolism* (Scribner's)

Abraham J. Heschel, *The Prophets* (HarperCollins)

Alan Jones, *Passion for Pilgrimage: Notes for the Journey Home* (HarperCollins)

Alan Jones, *Soul Making: The Desert Way of Spirituality* (HarperSanFrancisco)

Thomas R. Kelly, *A Testament of Devotion* (HarperSanFrancisco)

Sue Monk Kidd, *When the Heart Waits: Spiritual Direction for Life's Sacred Questions* (HarperCollins)

Anne Lamott, *Traveling Mercies: Some Thoughts on Faith* (Pantheon)

Thomas Merton, *Thoughts in Solitude* (Noonday Press)

Johannes B. Metz, *Poverty of Spirit* (Paulist)

Kathleen Norris, *Amazing Grace: A Vocabulary of Faith* (Riverhead)

Kathleen Norris, *The Cloister Walk* (Riverhead)

Kathleen Norris, *Dakota: A Spiritual Geography* (Mariner Books)

Henri J. M. Nouwen, *In the Name of Jesus: Reflections on Christian Leadership* (Crossroad)

Henri J. M. Nouwen, *The Inner Voice of Love: A Journey Through Anguish to Freedom* (Doubleday)

Henri J. M. Nouwen, *The Road to Daybreak: A Spiritual Journey* (Image)

Parker J. Palmer, *Let Your Life Speak: Listening for the Voice of Vocation* (Jossey-Bass)

Parker J. Palmer, *To Know As We Are Known: Education as a Spiritual Journey* (HarperSanFrancisco)

Eugene H. Peterson, *The Contemplative Pastor: Returning to the Art of Spiritual Direction* (Word)

Eugene H. Peterson, *Living the Message* (HarperCollins)

Eugene H. Peterson, *A Long Obedience in the Same Direction: Discipleship in an Instant Society* (InterVarsity Press)

Eugene H. Peterson, *Subversive Spirituality* (Eerdmans)

Barbara Brown Taylor, *The Preaching Life* (Cowley)

Barbara Brown Taylor, *When God Is Silent* (Cowley)

Evelyn Underhill, *The Spiritual Life* (Morehouse)

Evelyn Underhill, *The Ways of the Spirit* (Crossroad)

Dallas Willard, *The Spirit of the Disciplines: Understanding How God Changes Lives* (HarperSanFrancisco)

Philip Yancey, *The Jesus I Never Knew* (Zondervan)

Philip Yancey, *What's So Amazing about Grace?* (Zondervan)

STOP IMPERSONATING YOURSELF

Youth ministry is a glittering image full of highly visible programs, activities, and life-changing experiences. This makes it easy for youth ministers to dazzle parents and church members with their impact on young people. If you aren't careful, though, you become your program—fun, busy, energetic, passionate about God, confident—but with an inner life that is teeming with insecurities, doubt, and struggles with your faith. If truth is at the center of the gospel, then truth must also be at the center of you. If teenagers are demanding reality today (and they are), then reality starts with you.

• *ADMIT YOUR OWN BROKENNESS.* Not that you have to publicly list all of your sins, but you must somehow admit your own sinfulness and flaws. If you want your students to feel safe in youth group, then they need to know you're safe, flaws and all.

• *DON'T BE AFRAID TO ADMIT YOUR OWN STRUGGLES AND DOUBTS.* Your students won't be disappointed that you struggle; they'll recognize your faith in the middle of struggle and doubt.

• *HUMILITY IS THE FIRST SIGN OF GENUINE FAITH.* Too many youth workers talk down to young people, bludgeoning them with "you need to do this" and "unless you do that," and so on. They invariably use themselves as examples of commitment and dedication—despite the words of John the Baptizer: "He must increase, but I must decrease" (John 3:30, NASB). Your job isn't to impress teenagers with how spiritual you are, but with how faithful Jesus is. Your remarks about Jesus should always be sprinkled with gratitude.

• *LISTEN TO WHAT YOUR STUDENTS TELL YOU ABOUT THEIR WALKS WITH JESUS.* Don't teach them as though you're the only source of knowledge. Young people have much to teach *you* about Jesus.

• *THE CALL OF YOUTH MINISTRY IS ALL ABOUT JESUS.* Your passion and desire should be to constantly bring people to Jesus.

THE CLOSER YOU GET TO JESUS, THE LESS YOU KNOW

When I was 20, I knew everything about Jesus. I swaggered into high schools afraid of no one's arguments. The Bible was true, Jesus was God, and we all needed him. I still believe those things, but the swagger is more like a limp now. I know Jesus, but I don't know much about him. I love the Bible—it's even more true to me today than it was 40 years ago—but the truth I see now is much more complicated and mysterious. Jesus is very real to me, but he's also very elusive. Sometimes I wonder if I'm following him, or he's following me. Life has left its scars on me. My soul is thick and leathery, faded and torn, knocked around a lot. I'm not as sure about things as I used to be.

Yet here's the amazing part, the one absolute I cannot shake: Jesus.

As many times as I have disappointed him, as often as I have run from him, he hasn't given up on me. Every time I turn around, he's there. Every time I run from him, he's there.

I don't know as much about Jesus as I used to, but I do know one truth for sure: He's closer.

AUDIO AND VIDEO QUOTES AND NOTES

1. AUDIO—FINAL GENERAL SESSION AT THE YOUTH SPECIALTIES NATIONAL YOUTH WORKER'S CONVENTION. SAN FRANCISCO. 1986.

"The church is really messed up. The church is in really bad shape. But you know, it's all we've got."

"I hate to camp. Let me tell you why. I can't go to the bathroom. I get in one of those outhouses, and if I hear a squirrel, I'm through."

"It's the things you can't find in a book that really make a difference, that change a kid's life. The things you did accidentally. The things you did inadvertently."

This was the only recording of Dad that we could find before 1995. We found it saved in his filing cabinet. In some ways it's uncharacteristic of his speaking style. He's calm and slow-paced. Dad often got emotional in front of crowds, particularly at youth ministry conventions where he only slept a few hours each night. You can hear him struggling to hold back tears during the long silence at the beginning of the recording.

2. AUDIO—"FINDING GOD IN THE MIDST OF YOUR MINISTRY." NASHVILLE, TENNESSEE. 1995.

"Am I capable of being a revolutionary? I don't know.
But some of you are."

"$4,500 for a Popsicle? There'll be no more Popsicles
for this company!"

"How do you find God in the midst of your ministry?
Stop being afraid."

This talk takes place just two years after a life-changing retreat that Dad took with Henri Nouwen at the L'Arche Daybreak community outside of Toronto, Canada. You can hear Dad struggling to integrate his growing intimacy with Jesus into his own experience and understanding of ministry. Much of the language in this talk is borrowed from Nouwen's writings, although it was the developmentally disabled folks at L'Arche who really helped Dad get in touch with God's grace. The talk is lengthy; in future years he would work at making his talks shorter (notice the two video talks are each less then 25 minutes long). Highlights include "Yaconelli's Principles of Institutions" and a helpful set of points he calls "Where God Isn't in Your Ministry."

3. AUDIO—"GETTING FIRED FOR THE GLORY OF GOD." PITTSBURGH, PENNSYLVANIA. 2002.

"Hey, Charlie, shut up!"

"You stand up for what you believe, and then stuff just happens."

"What's happened in the church is that we have taught compliance."

This is one of our favorite talks. Dad is freewheeling, off-notes, spewing a stream-of-consciousness commentary on 40 years of ministry. A cell phone goes off, people heckle him from the audience, and yet he takes it all in and throws it right back out, daring people to live the gospel even if it means losing their jobs. "I'm qualified to teach this course," he declares, "because I've been fired at least twice." With the kind of energy he exerts in this seminar, you can believe it.

4. AUDIO—"DANGEROUS WONDER: CREATING A YOUTH MINISTRY MARKED BY DANGER." EDMONTON, ALBERTA, CANADA. 2003.

"You were concerned about kids in your church. You went to a meeting. You raised your hand to go to the bathroom, and now you're in charge."

"They said, 'Hey, Fanny, we want to do your funeral.' She said, 'That's great, but I'm not dead yet.'"

"Your youth program is basically you."

This is a talk in which you can hear a real connection with the youth working audience. At one point in this talk Dad reads some letters he's received from various youth workers. Dad often corresponded with youth workers. Sometimes he'd call up youth workers at their churches, and if they answered the phone he'd hassle them, saying, "Why are you in the office? Why aren't you hanging out with kids? Get out of the office. Next time I call, I want to get an answering machine."

5. DVD—FINAL GENERAL SESSION AT THE YOUTH SPECIALTIES NATIONAL YOUTH WORKER'S CONVENTION. NASHVILLE, TENNESSEE. 2002.

"I'm sorry…sort of."

"I can bring a deer in anytime."

"When the church decides it's a corporation,
we have to find a way to sabotage that."

The first thing we noticed when we watched this talk was the big rust sweater. Dad liked how he looked in sweaters. It would be 85 degrees outside, and he'd wear a sweater on stage. A few weeks before this talk he spent three days training in San Francisco to be an extra at Game 3 of the World Series. He ran onto the field with 20 other guys to hold up a sign marking the top-10 events of Major League Baseball. It was October in San Francisco, a night game. It was freezing. He wore a short -sleeve shirt.

This is one of the many closing talks Dad gave at the National Youth Worker's Convention. In each of these talks he tried to encourage youth workers to trust their instincts, embrace their calling, let go of their inhibitions, and give themselves to Jesus.

6. DVD—FINAL GENERAL SESSION AT THE YOUTH SPECIALTIES NATIONAL YOUTH WORKER'S CONVENTION. CHARLOTTE, NORTH CAROLINA. 2003.

"Routine deadens our imaginations."

"*Repent* means to take responsibility for my own deadness."

"When you speak the truth, when you present the gospel, and people aren't expecting it...then even Presbyterians who never clap, start clapping."

Notice the tucked-in shirt. He'd been on a diet for a few months and was happy about his new weight. His themes in this talk match much of the themes of his life—the struggle against routine, busyness, conventionality, and institutionalism. Two days after this talk he spent the day helping his father move into a new apartment. That evening as he drove home, he had some kind of cardiac event, swerved into a light pole, and passed into the next life.

Messy Spirituality

God's Annoying Love for Imperfect People

Michael Yaconelli

What if true spirituality couldn't be achieved by trying to live by some unrealistic standart of perfection that no one lives by anyway? What if there are no guaranteed guidelines, well-marked maps, or secrets to a "mature" faith? What if genuine spirituality is...well...messy? In *Messy Spirituality*, Mike Yaconelli encourages us to invite God into our lives—which will more readily lead to an authentic relationship with him as opposed to white-knuckling ourselves into the delusion that we first have to be okay before God accepts us. The result? Not perfect people, but people perfectly aware of the grace that God offers us every day of our lives.

Softcover: 978-0-310-27730-9

Pick up a copy today at your favorite bookstore!

These 30 devotions strip away the silliness, the buzz, and the hype of religion and deliver the truth on weakness, prepared-ness, hunger, fear, and more. This compilation of Scripture, story, and reflection is great for individuals or groups.

Devotion
A Raw-Truth Journal on Following Jesus
Mike Yaconelli
RETAIL $10.99
ISBN 978-0-310-25559-8